POLAR LANDSCAPES

A Multifaceted Historical Study

GARY LEE KVAMME

Volume 1

Telling Past Series

POLAR LANDSCAPES

A Multifaceted Historical Study

I

In late August, 1982, John Carpenter's *The Thing* opened in London theaters, introducing to British audiences some of the most grotesque and haunting special effects to date. The story depicted a team of Antarctic researchers who were brutally mutilated, digested, and seamlessly imitated by a 100,000 year old alien entity. Upon its initial release, both British and American critics remarked *The Thing* as gratuitous in its violence and downright depressing in its atmosphere.[1] One British reviewer claimed that the film would have audiences fleeing from the theater, crying "hell's bells, I've never seen anything like that before."[2] In a similar vein, a *New York Times* reviewer appealed, less favorably, that Carpenter used actors as mere "props to be hacked, slashed, disemboweled and decapitated, finally to be eaten and then regurgitated as more laboratory-concocted special effects."[3] Indeed, the film made a breakthrough in grotesque horror, costing nearly 1.5 million dollars in creature animatronics and costume design alone. It is the film's setting, however, particularly in its presentation of polar space, which is most notable in the context of this study.

The Thing, taking the 1938 John Campbell novella *Who Goes There?* as its source material, generated a scenario of polar nihilism. Throughout it were long shots of blanket white snow surrounded by bleak darkness, creating a sense of claustrophobia and isolation. This isolation became even more terrifying when the situation escalated to mass paranoia for the cast of researchers at Outpost 31. As the film progressed, Carpenter made clear that, between the polar wastes and the creature, the characters had no real chance for survival. By the end of the picture, MacReady (the film's protagonist) and Childs are the only members still alive. While Carpenter left their fate to ambiguity, the only real outcomes possible were: (1) they would be killed by "the thing" or (2) they would freeze to death in the Antarctic. As literary scholar Elena Glasberg remarked, the ending of *The Thing* presented a situation from which "no future can emerge."[4] She continued:

Neither science nor good-old American know-how prevails. Only a brutal containment can ensure the originality of humanity. Antarctica is again a grand terminus.[5]

In the above passage, Glasberg reflected that the setting itself was as much force of death as the creature found in it. The final lines of Bill Lancaster's script for the movie suggested this as well. They read: "The fires smolder on. Bright embers dance in the blackness—pushed by the soughing wind."[6] The last scene, depicting dancing embers

2

"in the blackness," created the sense of polar nihilism earlier mentioned. As Lancaster's script suggested, the embers will eventually burn out, and MacReady and Childs (if they are both *actually* MacReady and Childs), having exhausted all possible escapes, will undoubtedly freeze to death. From the start, the leading characters were doomed in their chances for survival. Even with the creature dead, the larger problem of the Antarctic landscape would surely finish doing what "the thing" could not.

In such a film, Carpenter used the Antarctic as a catalyst for horror. In his reimagining of Campbell's novella, the American director presented for viewers a story human characters, who, as he related in a *Times* interview, were entirely "trapped...and have lost control of the given situation."[7] The setting created a sense of isolation that inevitably ended in nihilism, leaving its title characters hopeless in the face of a landscape that would inevitably swallow them. At its core, *The Thing* was an apocalyptic story about close quarters in a massively expansive (and empty) landscape. Themes of isolation, terror, and death were paramount as men like MacReady were forced to face a situation that brought out the worst in humanity, whether it be through psychological or literal means.

Such a film as Carpenter's works well as an illustration of how polar space was imagined in late twentieth-century American and English culture. The Antarctic was a place to tell stories of isolation, survival, death, heroics, and terror. It was (and still is) a catalyst used by both

Europeans and Americans to talk about human failure in alien landscapes. There was no triumph in stories like *The Thing*—there was not even a hope for survival. The only thing its characters could hope for was containment.

Indeed, such depictions have multiple historical and literary counterparts. Early twentieth-century depictions, namely those by H.P. Lovecraft, John Martin Leahy, and John Campbell, all influenced this terrifying and desolate imagining of the Antarctic. In *Who Goes There?*, the novella that served as Carpenter's primary source for *The Thing*, the landscape was related as having a "white death" color that sucked heat and life with its "needle-fingered cold."[8] The Antarctic, as depicted in the early science fiction literary imaginings was a space of endless white mist, covering both sky and land with fine particles of snow that "obscured all things."[9]

This study follows British polar exploration from the early nineteenth century to the early twentieth century, highlighting its chief explorers and literary figures. While historians like William Mills cited that polar expeditions ranged back as far as 325 BC, the timeframe discussed throughout this paper focuses primarily on the Imperial British experience in the Arctic and Antarctic.[10] Beginning around 1818, just years after the Napoleonic wars, the first Arctic expeditions were led by British naval officer John Franklin. These expeditions, which promised both scientific and economic benefits, were centered on the exploration of the northern Canadian coastlines and the search for the Northwest Passage.

Much of Arctic exploration during the first half of the nineteenth century were naval endeavors that, as literary scholar Chauncey Loomis argued, demonstrated the belief that "British manhood and British power were on the line in the continued search for the passage."[11] Sir John Barrow, who was serving as secretary to the British Admiralty during the mid-Victorian period, provided a notable example of this in his letters to the British people. In 1844, Barrow addressed the mainland with a heartfelt appeal to continue the search of the Northwest Passage. He wrote:

A final attempt to make a north-west passage would render the most important service that now remains to be performed towards the completion of the magnetic survey of the globe; and its hardly necessary to say, that the geography and hydrography of this part of the Polar Sea would be a valuable addition to our knowledge of the globe, and well deserving the attention of a power like England.[12]

He continued to relate that if England allowed the passage to be discovered by another world power, then "England by her neglect of it...would be laughed at by all the world."[13] As Barrow argued in his letters, Arctic expeditions in this period were connected to imperial gains as well as commercial. The fear that England "would be laughed at by all the world," and its response to prove the opposite, played a significant role in the expeditions from 1818 to 1845.[14]

More than ever, the English mainland celebrated Northern exploration as a national sensation. Due to the industrial revolution, the printing press was finally coming into its own, publishing newspapers and books at a previously unmatched rate. In effect, many of explorer narratives were published and edited by booksellers like John Murray, an English publisher who also played a substantial role in the distribution of books like Jane Austen's Emma and Lord Byron's *Childe Harolde's Pilgrimage.*[15] Newspapers like *The Times*, *The Daily Mirror*, and *The Illustrated London News* also contributed to such publications, all the while adamantly supporting the Admiralty in its continual organization of polar expeditions.[16] For example, in defense of the many polar exploits operating throughout the 1800s, *The Illustrated London News* claimed that "an instinct or a passion for maritime exploration lay at the very root...of British nature."[17] Passages like these, by linking "British nature" to exploration itself, helped to generate a great deal of interest in polar exploits and their relation to English identity.

British interest in the Arctic and Northwest Passage, however, would eventually be culled by the continual failures and explorer disappearances surrounding the journeys North, reaching a peak at the reported death of Franklin in 1854. While the search for the Northwest Passage set the tone for such endeavors, it was its underlying themes, those of English manhood, heroism, and intellectual superiority, that would serve as the justification for further expeditions to the South Pole.

Cited by historians as the Heroic Age of Antarctic Exploration, this period of polar exploration ranged primarily from the 1890s to 1920.[18] More so than the Arctic expeditions, Imperial Britain's chief interest in the Antarctic was founded in nationalistic rivalries, primarily between the Norwegians and Germans.19 English explorers like Ernest Shackleton and Robert Falcon Scott played key roles in the renewed race to the South Pole. Although similar in purpose, these expeditions, the chief among them being the *Terra Nova*, *Discovery*, and the *Endurance*, were largely private endeavors. Unlike Arctic explorers like Franklin, who had the financial backing of the British Admiralty, explorers like Shackleton had to turn to the Royal Geographical Society and private donors for funding.[20] Though a similar outcome of failure and death became a recurring theme throughout expeditions South, the failures of explorers like Scott and Shackleton were memorialized by the press and English public as heroic sacrifices, proving that: even if the British could not win the race to the South Pole, they were still able to attest superiority through hardship, endurance, and martyrdom.

The narratives produced by such exploits serve as the primary backbone of this study. From the explorers' descriptions of the Arctic and Antarctic, a plethora of artistic and literary reinterpretations followed. And these reinterpretations, like the cultural climate of Britain, changed throughout the nineteenth and twentieth centuries. While the twentieth-century imaginings of the South Pole depicted a much more dangerous, harsh, and monstrous landscape, the nineteenth-century representations of authors and explorers imagined such spaces as beautiful, heroic, and even intellectually edifying. For example, authors like Mary Shelley, in her famous novel *Frankenstein*, saw the North Pole as offering the "greatest consolation," elevating the onlooker to enlightenment itself.[21] Similarly, English explorer George Back depicted the Canadian Arctic as "a stranger combination of ruin and confusion with the softness and harmony of the most beautiful tints."[22] Both interpretations, from author and explorer, represent a largely different polar space than the twentieth-century imaginings of Campbell and Carpenter. In these illustrations, the English mainland imagined polar space as romantically sublime, representing both ruin and consolation, enlightenment and harmony.

Such sources, including both fictional and nonfictional representations of the Arctic and Antarctic, varied throughout the Victorian and modern period. English polar explorers like John Franklin, George Back, Ernest Shackleton, and Robert Falcon Scott were the primary contributors to these sublime representations. In addition, authors like Mary Shelley, Jules Verne, and Edgar Allen Poe contributed to the collective public imagination through their own fantastical stories in the poles. The infusion of polar and literary narrative did more than relate the Arctic and Antarctic to the English. Indeed, it was largely responsible for fashioning the poles into a quasi-mythological space that allowed for the Empire's own expression (or proving) of mid-Victorian conceptions of masculinity, heroism, and intellectual superiority. Thus, the landscape, which was seen by only a select few explorers, whether they were British, German, American, or Scandinavian, became a contested space in its representation by both public and imperial agents, changing greatly from the mid-nineteenth to early twentieth century.

At the peak of the British Empire's power, ranging from around 1860 to 1890, the representations of the poles were sublimely wondrous, pristine, and illuminating.[23] As modernism and the Great War approached into the collective mind of the public, however, the landscape had changed to better suit the needs of Empire. Rather than "messengers of daring art," the explorers became martyrs, performing their duty "to the last," who were nearly worshiped by the English for their sacrifice at the far corners of the earth.[24]

This study is hinged upon a shifting conception of the Sublime—from Victorian to modern, from nineteenth-century romanticism to twentieth-century pessimism. It is ultimately a study of the British Empire during a time of decline and how this aesthetic concept operated in both conjunction and disjunction throughout this period. While the Sublime is a concept typically explored in literary scholarship, its historical importance is evident in the way that the English represented spaces like the poles. Nineteenth-century British culture was a very literary one. Events, whether related by the press, politicians, or authors, were usually remembered and stylized by the British through an elite literary language.[25] Polar discourse works as a testament to such an interpretive and literary period's reflection on its own time. From the mainland perspective, artist and newspapers worked tirelessly to represent the landscape described by explorers like George

Back. For example, publications from *The Illustrated London News* frequently printed engravings of Arctic exploration, allowing its readers to imagine what Northern exploration might look like. Indeed, even polar explorers like Douglas Mawson and Ernest Shackleton produced their own poetry and fictional stories inspired by their experiences in the far North or South.

The language of the Sublime, as related by both explorers and authors, was a reoccurring theme throughout many polar retellings. In a sense, the North and South "mapped" by polar explorers was a fictional copy of their actual experiences. Arctic explorers worked very carefully to depict an aesthetic map of the North, often leaving out the harsher details of polar space in favor of depicting it as imaginative and astonishing.[26] For example, Back, in several publications, worked with Victorian publisher John Murray to produce a text about the Arctic that was "replete with danger and novelty."[27] Murray, who had published material by authors like Lord Byron, Jane Austen, and Herman Melville, often required Back to provide several drafts before publishing the actual narrative.[28] These drafts were an infusion of actual polar experiences and a carefully crafted literary language. In effect, understanding the literary (Sublime) context of polar discourse becomes a key tool in understanding its historical context.

The Sublime, which started as an aesthetic philosophy carefully molded by European intellectuals like Edmund Burke and Immanuel Kant, had ultimately become a way that Victorian high society categorized and imagined uninhabitable landscapes. From Romantics like Lord

Byron and William Wordsworth, who imagined Europe's mountains and valleys as sublime, to English explorers like George Back and Ernest Shackleton, who saw polar space through this aesthetic lens, the Sublime had become a higher form of visual taste defined by characteristics of great wonder and terror. The quest then, taken upon by British explorers, was to map the empty and alien, uninhabitable spaces of the globe and give them an identity that was fundamentally British. These spaces became Sublime.

From the Sublime, themes of romanticism, terror, and heroism emerge. While the early publications about the Arctic depicted the landscape as a wonder-filled mystery, the later nineteenth-century depictions, following continual reports of privation and death in the North, shifted the English imagining of the landscape, emphasizing the terrible realities that polar travels could inflict upon those who ventured there. The late nineteenth and early-twentieth century expedition retellings of the Arctic, and primarily the Antarctic, depicted a landscape in a much more pessimistic light, fitting it firmly into a modern context. In such a context, the Antarctic, as related by both explorers and their interpreters, became an antagonistic space. Men like Shackleton and Scott were remembered by the English as performing "warfare" in the polar wastes, ultimately associating British heroism with the Southern-most convenient.[29] In effect, the way that polar discourse progressed historically was significantly founded upon the way that the literary environment changed in its understanding of these spaces. First they were wonderful, then terrible, and finally they provided the British with a kind of proof that the men who died there were the truest heroes that a culture could hope for.[30]

Before examining Polar exploration and its role in this study, it is important to look at the cultural climate of nineteenth- and twentieth-century Europe. By the 1860s, the Victorian age was defined by its industrial prosperity.[31] The Empire had experienced a "head start" in the industrial revolution, and was producing products so great in number that new markets had to be established for it to profit off of them.[32] Due to such material wealth, England began to expand its formal colonial presence on the global stage, scrambling against other nations to carve up locations in Africa and Asia.[33] The acquisition of new territories, as historian Geoffrey Barraclough put it, was primarily to "safe-guard existing possessions or to prevent the control of strategic routes passaging into the hands of other powers."[34] In effect, British economic thinking was centered on colonies both supplying the home front with raw materials for manufacturing and providing a market for the distribution of such goods.[35] For the Empire to profit, it had to be the only distributor to its colonies.

National rivalries also played a role in mid-Victorian imperial expansion. By the 1870s, Germany, France, and the United States were beginning to make their way in the global market.[36] Indeed, Germany had already begun to compete with Britain in naval and industrial strength, and France had begun to regain its own standing on the global stage.[37] At the start of this new colonial push, Europe controlled about 7% of the world's population.[38] However, by the 1900s, 84% of the world was controlled by various European powers—25% being British.[39] Such imperial expansion was, of course, reflected on a cultural level. For example, in her children's poem, titled "An ABC for Baby Patriots," Mary Francis Ames wrote:

C is for Colonies

Rightly we boast,

That of all the great nations,

Great Britain has most.[40]

Indeed, Ames' claim that "Great Britain has most" was a reality by the end of the nineteenth century. As historian Timothy Parsons noted in *The British Imperial Century*, the British Empire had expanded nearly 10 million square miles during its nineteenth-century phase of colonial expansion.[41] The twentieth century, however, would usher in a specter of decline for the Empire. Cited by historians like Geoffrey Barraclough, Timothy Parson, and John M. Mackenzie as New Imperialism, this European colonial push had three primary motivations: economic growth, political competition, and racial superiority.[42]

Being that this study's primary focus is on Britain's cultural environment from the 1860s to 1920s, it is important to examine the social effects of New Imperialism, which had been accelerated by the "unbridled imperial Victorian optimism" of the mid-nineteenth century.[43] As Charles Kinsley, an English historian and clergyman, related, it was the British privilege and God-given right to "replenish and subdue" the world.[44] This mid-Victorian mindset saw the British as intellectually superior to the "uncivilized" spaces of the world. Thus, British conceptions of virtue, heroism, and masculinity became the mode of imperial representation abroad. Because other non-English cultures did not express concepts of Victorian stoicism, masculinity, self-control, and, above all, duty, it became the burden of the British to educate them.[45]

The British desire to enlighten the non-English world was also manifested in literary representations. Authors like Charles Dickens, Rudyard Kipling, and Thomas Carlyle all contributed to the nationalistic teachings coming out of this period.[46] For example, Kipling, who was referred to by English novelist George Orwell as "the prophet of British Imperialism in its expansionist phase," claimed that the colonized were "sullen peoples, half-devil and half-child."[47] Coming from an excerpt of "The White Man's Burden," Kipling's referral of those under British rule worked as a prime example of the British notion of self-superiority, seeing other peoples as cruel and without the virtue of moral reasoning. Another example of Britain's belief in its own supremacy was depicted in the letters of English historian Thomas Arnold, who, while touring Southern France observed that the English were a "greater people than these [the French]," concluding that they were indeed "one of the chosen people of history who are appointed to do great work for mankind."[48] Similarly, Kinsley claimed that that the English had been given, by god, the "glorious work" of replenishing and subduing the world.[49] Arnold and Kinsley's observations about the

Empire during the nineteenth century were typical of their age. As historian John M. MacKenzie put it: "the British basked in their imperial glory and developed a powerful notion of their own superiority."[50]

While the mid-nineteenth century brought a great deal of colonial expansion and cultural confidence to Victorian Britain, the twentieth century would usher in a specter of decline for the Empire.[51] The political disaster of the Boer War, followed by The Great War, would consequently bring about a great loss in Britain's overseas territory, permanently quelling the Victorian optimism displayed in the mid-Victorian period. Of the Boer War, historian Dane Kennedy, in *Britain and Empire*, argued that "no event was more responsible for raising doubts about the nation's future."[52] The war itself was fought by the British against the Transvaal Republic, also known as the Afrikaners, and Orange Free State. While Britain claimed that the war was to achieve strategic national interests, being that the Afrikaners had connections to Germany, the popular historical analysis is that Britain was also fighting for control of gold mines in Transvaal.[53] Although the war was an eventual success, it would prove a moral and economic disaster for Britain. By 1902, the Empire had spent 230 million pounds and engaged 450,000 troops against some 70,000 Boers.[54] Indeed, party leaders like Henry Campbell-Bannerman questioned the very foundations of the war itself, asking rhetorically "When is a war not a war?," only to answer moments later: "When it is carried on by methods of barbarism in South Africa."[55] In likening British imperial endeavors to "barbarism," the

Liberal Party leader questioned the intellectual foundations of the British imperial project—namely those concerning the Empire's moral superiority.

There was an even more gruesome side to the Boer War, however. In order to encourage the South African soldiers to surrender, the British had the wives and children of the Afrikaners put into concentration camps. This was met with general disapproval from a number of English citizens. For example, British welfare campaigner Emily Hobhouse, when aiding the South Africans who had been captured by British soldiers, called the Empire's arrangement "a wholesale cruelty."[56] She continued:

To keep these Camps going is murder to the children…It is such a curious position, hollow and rotten to the heart's core, to have made all over the State large uncomfortable communities of people whom you call refugees and say you are protecting, but who call themselves prisoners of war, compulsorily detained, and detesting your protection. They are tired of being told by officers that they are refugees under *the kind and beneficent protection of the British*.[57]

Hobhouse's emphasis on "the kind and beneficent protection of the British" captured the critical atmosphere of the Boer War on the home front. As Hobhouse related, the *"beneficent protection"* of the British ultimately led to the murder of innocent children, the elderly, and women. Over 28,000 died in the British concentration camps, the majority being children sixteen and younger.[58] Such a death toll weighed heavily on the public's conscience, sparking many debates concerning the effectiveness and

16

legacy of Britain's empire.[59] For example, Lloyd David George, during a dispute in parliament, criticized British military policy, claiming that:

When children are being treated in this way and dying, we are simply ranging the deepest passions of the human heart against British rule in Africa. The love of men for their children, for their home, for their country, and for humanity—we are ranging all these passions against settled government under the British flag in Africa. It will always be remembered that this is the way British rule started here, and this is the method by which it was brought about.[60]

The statesman's argument lends insight into the political environment during and following the Boer war. The question of British rule and its legacy had entered the public conscience. This question, mingled with the new waves of feminism and the continual rise of political rivals like Germany, caused a great deal of anxiety for Imperialist Britain. In effect, the need to prove the Empire's ethical values grew even more pressing during the early twentieth century.

The late nineteenth-century anxiety expressed by Imperial British culture is explored throughout the bulk of this work. In effect, polar exploration and its development of polar heroes went hand in hand with the doubt (in the imperial project) that the British public felt after events like the Boer War. In addition, the progression of women's suffrage called into question traditional concepts of Victorian masculinity and gender. Norms of gender and morality, which had come to represent the rhythm of everyday life, were thrown into flux at the dawn of the modern world. By the time that reports of Scott and Shackleton's death in the Antarctic had reached the public, Imperial British culture had begun a project that sought to reclaim the orthodox forms of Victorian virtues, reminding the public that the Britishness of old still existed in their Empire.

This reaffirmation of orthodox Britishness played a significant role in twentieth-century polar exploration. Due to this renewed desire to present English heroes to the public, explorers of the late nineteenth and early twentieth centuries were represented by British high society as archetypes of manliness, heroism, and endurance. While the British usually celebrated these men as heroes, to one degree or another, the press and politicians alike used stories of their exploits as a rallying point for British imperial culture. Scholars like Dane Kennedy, Paul Carter, and Mary Lewis Pratt all examine the discursive practices surrounding this point of exploration history.

My study, in its use of literary sources and concepts (like the Sublime), polar narratives, and press coverage, works as a cultural history of British polar exploration. The methodologies presented by Pratt, Kenney, and Carter, which interpret explorer efforts (whether intentional or unintentional) as "tied to imperial ambitions," are used as a starting point, viewing the discourse surrounding expeditions as allowing the English to take ownership of space, ultimately transforming the landscapes and those who went there into token examples of mid-Victorian Britishness.[61]

The final portion of this section will examine the historiographical scholarship surrounding polar studies, followed by a layout of my own study and its place in the academic field. While scholars occasionally categorize polar studies under the larger branch of exploration history, it differs in its approach to landscapes (being that the poles were largely uninhabited). Throughout much of this scholarship, the landscape itself becomes Other, rather than native peoples. Although British spatial claim was still the object, claiming polar space became particularly linguistic, favoring aesthetic and literary forms of ownership rather than physical occupation. Ultimately, it is a story about the English explorers, the public imagination, and the polar landscape. The English exploits in the polar regions was consequently a discursive analysis, using the literary circulation, from explorer to public, from public to explorer, to claim ownership.

There are several ways that this study complements and contends with the current body of polar scholarship. Throughout the following sections, I show how British literary culture directly influenced the way that events and spaces were remembered and documented historically. Being that polar discourse was significantly dependent on the literary representations of the Arctic and Antarctic, both American and European authors like Verne, Shelley, Lovecraft, and Poe helped to contribute to polar space's imaging as Sublime, providing insight into its shift from Victorian Romanticism to Modernism. Secondly, this study shows a direct relation between the discourse surrounding the modern world, the Antarctic, and the First

World War. As historian Paul Fussell cited in The Great War in Modern Memory, there can be no World War discourse without the literary representations of it.[62] In the same way, my own research shows that there can be no polar discourse without the authors who contributed to it. The mythologizing of the North and South Poles worked in a very similar way as The Great War and its war poets. Indeed, the same themes are even present in the conception of the No Man's Land, which was ultimately a sublime, indescribable space of fascination during World War I.

The historiographical scholarship itself ranges from the study of individual explorers, such as Ernest Shackleton, Douglas Mawson, and John Franklin, to an inquiry of motives, concerning nations, romanticism, aesthetics, and imperialism. Polar studies, in the context of history and literary scholarship, is relatively new to the academic world. Being more reliant on the discourse surrounding the Arctic and Antarctic, much of the early academic focus was forwarded by literary scholars, who took great interest in the aesthetic imagings of such spaces. Ultimately, this branch of polar studies sought to explain the way that the imperial discourse surrounding the poles worked as a way of claiming them, turning them from a foreign and alien landscape to a space that could be conquered and unlocked only through the intellectual tools and aesthetic learning of the British.

Since its separation from Canadian scholarship and literary studies, polar studies has expanded into the broader umbrella of postcolonial, cultural, and imperial history. In effect, the scholarship surrounding the poles and their discursive practices is slowly gaining more of a foothold in academic circles. The labors of scholars writing about nineteenth-century polar exploration are particularly concerned with two themes: 1) how the forces of Empire created the desire and environment for Arctic and Antarctic exploration and 2) how the effects of such exploration changed both the culture at home and abroad. In a broader prospect, alongside questions of decline, race, and identity, this forms one of the key themes in the scholarship surrounding imperialism. While this study, in its examination of the cultural climate of Britain, fits more in the second category, both categories ultimately situate the historiography of polar exploration, contextualizing it as part of the larger approach to studies of Empire.

Early studies concerning these regions were typically associated with the Arctic and Canadian history, ultimately finding their start in the fields of literary scholarship. Being that scholars from this period were heavily focused and reliant on the narrative of explorers who braved the North, much of the early publications focused on British Admiral John Franklin's ill-fated expedition to the Arctic. Canadian academics, such as Ian MacLaren and Michael Krans, primarily worked with the narratives provided by explorers who partook in these expeditions, showing how such texts created the space of the Arctic, turning the landscape into an aesthetic, marketable, and English phenomenon. In his article "The Aesthetic Map of the North," MacLaren noted that much of the language used to describe the Arctic was part of a campaign to make the landscape familiar to the British, ultimately making a "garden of the desert" and "decoding the inscrutable sublimities of the terrain."[63] Such a way of describing the vast northern spaces "provided the nineteenth-century imperialist with a way to make other parts of the globe British," argued MacLaren, claiming that "the Picturesque and the Sublime dictated how the terrain was perceived," revealing to the English readers where they stood in relation to the natural world.[64]

In addition to MacLaren, the scholarship of Michael Krans worked to set the stage for much of polar studies to follow. Krans, like MacLaren, examined the way that the explorers relate the Arctic to the English people. In his essay, titled "Writing for an Elsewhere," Krans argued that the landscape which British explorers like Franklin presented was "fundamentally inauthentic."[65] Taking note that these explorers "refused to present the Arctic as it appeared to their own eyes, as it emerged in their own embodied experience," the Canadian scholar ultimately claimed that many British explorers died because they refused to see the landscape through the eyes of those (more experienced peoples) who were not part of the Empire.[66] Such scholarship as Krans' and MacLaren's paved the way for later postcolonial and cultural studies to come. By taking the narratives and examining the refusal of English explorers to see or relate the *authentic* Arctic, these scholars set the stage of an examination of polar discourse that would expand far beyond literary studies, further bringing the field of polar studies into the larger world of cultural and imperial history.

As more articles were published in Canadian journals like *Arctic*, British literary scholars began adding to the academic discourse, focusing primarily on the English reaction to the deaths of John Franklin and his crew. One of the major themes running through the early Arctic scholarship circulated on the refusal of the British to come to terms with the dangerous reality of the poles. British literary scholars Ian Stone and James Marlow addressed this issue by examining the reaction of Victorian author Charles Dickens to the death and supposed cannibalism of Franklin and his shipwrecked crew. In their articles, titled "The contents of the Kettles" and "English Cannibalism," Marlow and Stone acknowledged the revulsion and denial that Dickens felt when hearing the possibility of Englishmen turning cannibal. Both articles focused on the roots of such denial, for Dickens and the English as a whole. Marlow wrote:

Franklin stood for the ideal balance of English civilization: courage with kindness, energy with self-discipline. If he could be brought to the level of the lowest savage in a vain struggle for survival, there would be no hope that normal Englishmen would not choose to survive at whatever cost.[67]

Such a passage examined the consequences of an English hero falling to the "savagery" of cannibalism. In addition, this realization meant that Western civilization, as represented by the English, was shown to be no different from the "uncivilized worlds" that it sought to enlighten.[68]

While Marlow and James were able to bring polar studies back to the field of British literary studies, their

23

articles focused very little on the reaction of the public as a whole, as well as the broader story to be told in relation to Arctic and Antarctic expeditions. The more recent scholarship, particularly articles and books published by historian Francis Spufford, focused more on the commercial and public interest in these spaces. For example, Spufford, in *I May Be Some Time*, traced the changing depictions of the Arctic and Antarctic, examining how, as the public received and fictionalized the landscape, the actual interpretation became more psychologically and metaphorically charged during the continuation of expeditions in the early twentieth century. *I May Be Some Time*, a title referencing a quote from the Antarctic explorer Robert Falcon Scott, stood as one of the first books in polar studies to make the transition from the Arctic to Antarctic. While the North and South poles are vastly different in numerous aspects, the discourse surrounding each were largely the same. The English approach to both the geographical spaces, in its aesthetic sensibilities and refusal to acknowledge the authentic landscape, drew from and produced much of the same public reaction and commercial fascination. While imperialism was a theme running throughout books and articles by Marlow, James, and Spufford, much of the English scholarship to this point took the perspective of polar exploration as entertainment or in reference to literary figures, seeing it as a commercial endeavor rather than a kind of imperial conquest through geography.

This study deviates from this historiographical trend, ultimately taking into account the effects that polar discursive practices had on claiming the North and South. Explorers were still imperial figures. While the poles could not provide a physical presence for the British to operate, those who went there were still practicing imperialism by claiming space through knowledge about it. Indeed, it was the British, not the Inuit (in the Arctic's case), that had the rhetorical and intellectual proficiencies to make geographical, scientific, and aesthetic claims about polar space—conquering it through literary, if not physical, means.

The most recent scholarship involving the poles emphasized the explorer narratives and their relation to Victorian society, further showing how romanticism, nation-building, and masculinity worked in juxtaposition with one another to shape the way that the world was understood by the English during the nineteenth century. In effect, these narratives provided not only a story about the spaces they explored, but a window into the workings of Imperial Britain itself. Historians like Felix Driver, Matthew Edney, and Paul Carter interwove studies in nineteenth-century exploration with imperial studies, making explicit the connection between imperialism and the commercial interest of mapping during the nineteenth century. By taking the narratives of the explorers, these historians were able to show how claims about science and space were used to elevate the British as the authority on such spaces.

The books and articles of scholars like Edward Said and Michel Foucault work well to enrich this later portion of polar scholarship. Foucault's article, titled "Question on

Geography," brought to attention the relation between power and knowledge about a particular space. He wrote:

Once knowledge can be analyzed in terms of region, domain, implantation, displacement, transposition, one is able to capture the process by which knowledge functions as a form of power and disseminates the effects of power.[69]

Such a statement served as an antidote for the particular way that the English were claiming the poles during the nineteenth century. By refusing to accept the harsh realities of these locales, in favor of an intellectualized aesthetic imagining, the English were able to create a discourse that they believed unlocked the secrets to such places, in effect holding dominion over them. In producing a great deal of literature about these places, they effectively pushed an image into the way that people thought about them.

In addition to Foucault, Edward Said's *Orientalism* introduced the concept of geographical imagining. This concept argued that, through the use of exploration narrative, the English turned foreign landscapes into savage, untamed worlds in need of civilization; in their recreation of the Orient, the British created a space that could justify imperialism. Imaginative geography "legitimates a vocabulary," wrote Said, it created and authenticated a "universe of representative discourse" unique to what is said and understood about a given space.[70] In effect, what explorers like Back or Shackleton reflected to readers about polar space, contributed to a growing body of discourse surrounding it. Such a discourse, with its infusion of explorer narratives, literary imaginings, artistic depictions, and press coverage, became more real (for the English public) than the actual, physical location. Works like Said's ultimately became the backbone for the most recent scholarship concerning the polar regions, allowing scholars to look at the narratives provided by the explorers, the fictionalized accounts written by the literary class, and the response of the public to these fantastical imaginings, as a form of discourse directly related to imperialism.

Using the foundation laid by Said and Foucault, historians Matthew Edney and Felix Driver showed how nineteenth-century explorers worked as imperial agents, functioning to control spaces by making scientific and geographical claims about them. In *Geography Militant*, Driver argued that the Royal Geographic Society and its many expeditions worked as a "base for imperial science."[71] By scientifically categorizing and naming objects, locales, and species, the British were effectively able to claim ownership over such spaces. In a similar vein, Edney's *Mapping the Empire* added to this assumption, asking key questions like: "What is the area of overlap between the ideology of map-making and the ideology of empire."[72] By looking at the East India Company's cartographical surveys and ideals, Edney was able to show how the British emphasis on science, empirical observation, and categorization helped to define India as Other. The British "had science, the Indians did not," wrote Edney, concluding that cartography was a scientific activity, and thus a British activity.[73] Such an implication made a hierarchy of knowledge, placing the

Empire at the top of the ladder. While historians like Driver and Edney did not deal with the Arctic and Antarctic directly, their works served to enrich the field of polar studies, providing methodologies that could easily carry over into the scholarly discourse surrounding such spaces.

In addition to geographical and scientific claims about space, historian Paul Carter argued that the narratives of explorers sought to define spaces largely through rhetorical, European standards. While such endeavors did not seek to make a material presence for the Empire, the intellectual presence claimed these spaces as British. For Carter, exploration was a deliberate contemplation, created with the desire for the explorer's own prestige and that of his nations'.[74] In the world of the imperial explorer, the new landscape "was a rhetorical construction, a product of language and the intentional gaze, not of the detached, dictionary clasping spectator."[75] The discourse created by such expeditions was a discourse of power, fueled by rhetorical language and representation. Such imaginative representations were used by the explorers who wittingly (or unwittingly) recreated such spaces to fit English standards. In effect, works like Carter's and Edney's fit well into the historiographical discussion, situating the many narratives of polar explorers in the imperial context.

Another major theme in the historiography is centered on how imperial endeavors like exploration helped to reflect, create, and alter English identities. While works like Lina Colley's *Britons* aren't directly related to the polar historiography, they serve to better shape our understanding of the imperial context in which polar exploration took place. For example, *Britons* looked at national identity in Britain, arguing it to be a thing of invention, fueled and forged by war, religion, trade, and empire.[76] In addition, the scholarship of Kathleen Wilson, Graham Dawson, and Jonathan Rutherford revealed the multivalent and shifting gender formations in the Empire, calling into question the stability of British identity itself. Such writings delve into themes of gender, exploration, and colonization, examining how language, in both the literature and narratives of nineteenth-century expeditions, ultimately played a major role in not only the creation and gendering of foreign spaces, but in the creation and gendering of national identities.

In Kathleen Wilson's *The Island Race*, the primary themes surfacing delved into "the heterogeneous and unstable nature of national identity in eighteenth-century Britain and its first empire."[77] At the core of Wilson's study was an exploration of "the impact of empire and gender on productions of national identity and its failures."[78] Throughout the book, she examined the performativity of the nation in the context of class, gender, and race.[79] In effect, she destabilized national British identity by showing it to be a "site of struggle," greatly influenced by the "Otherness" that it sought to separate itself from.[80] While Wilson's work reinforced earlier assumptions made by in Colley's *Britons*, the emphasis on social performance, how identities were "understood, performed, and consumed," drew a connection between British identity and the body, linking the historiography of empire to more theoretical studies of gender presented by philosophers like Judith Butler.[81] Such works fit well into polar historiography. Throughout the nineteenth and twentieth centuries, polar space had been transformed by the English into a space to perform heroics, masculinity, and intellectual superiority. In a period where British identity had become a "site of struggle," landscapes like the Arctic and Antarctic were used by the Empire to prove the existence and worth of mid-Victorian conceptions of Britishness.

In addition to Wilson's work on empire and gender, Graham Dawson's *Soldier Heroes* and Jonathan Rutherford's *Forever England* delved into examinations of various forms of expressed masculinity in the nineteenth and twentieth centuries. By looking at the lives and writings of men like T.E. Lawrence, David Livingstone, and Rupert Brooke, these authors take into account new masculinities created by popularized adventure stories and romanticized imaginings of the imperial soldier-hero. Rutherford, in *Forever England*, ultimately traced and explained the contention found between nineteenth- and twentieth-century explorers and boyhood domesticity. This contention, he concluded, led many of these explorers to travel and express their own masculinity thousands of miles away from the English mainland.

Following such publications, literary scholar Jen Hill issued *White Horizon: The Arctic in the Nineteenth-Century British Imagination*, which examined the ways that gender formation worked alongside the imperial discourse created by polar exploration. Such a work tied polar explorations to gender formations, finding many similarities in the claims made by Wilson and Colley. Such publications worked to expand the historiographical field beyond imperial studies and into gender studies.

Although polar studies, at least in the historical context, is a relatively new field, it has changed much in its academic life. Moving from Canadian history and literary studies to studies in imperialism, the future of the field seems to rest in further assimilating it into the larger field of imperial and cultural history. While the most recent scholarship has progressed into gender studies, there is still very little said about the large body of narratives provided by the explorers themselves, from Arctic explorers like George Back to late nineteenth-century and early twentieth-century explorers like Shackleton, Scott, and Mawson. Concerning my own research in polar exploration, the defining methodology begins with books like *Orientalism* and *Road to Botany Bay*, drawing from studies in postcolonialism, British identity, and gender. By dividing the research into three parts, (roughly) the Sublime, terror, and heroism, my research explores a number of the same themes found in works like *The Island Race*, *Mapping the Empire*, and *I May Be Some Time*. The Antarctic and Arctic expeditions are, although different in execution, still a story about Empire, divided and defined more sharply into categories of ownership, identity, and decline. These categories help to tell a reactionary story of imperial degeneration in a modernizing context. The language used, both to make the poles sublime and to scientifically *conquer* them, worked to create a sense of

Otherness in the landscape, making it into a foreign world that only the English could define. In the same way that Edney showed how the British emphasis on mapping and science defined a stronger line between the Empire and India, one of this study's key objectives is to show how imperial identity was not only defined in relation to foreign peoples, but to foreign landscapes (which were in some sense the last spaces for such performances of imperial masculinity and ethics). By using the poles as a catalyst to better outline the qualities of Englishness, Imperial Britain was able to create in them a space that reflected mid-Victorianism, transforming the landscape to contend with modernism and decline.

This thematic transformation of the Arctic and Antarctic works well as the layout for this study, dividing polar exploration into two distinct phases—the first focusing particularly on the Romantic Sublime, which was categorized primarily by interpreting the Canadian North as pristine, indescribable, and filled with wonder. The second phase examines the Modern Sublime, which depicted the Antarctic as a wasteland, defined by themes of privation, desolation, and obscurity. This shift, from Sublime wonder to terror was expressed by both fictional and nonfictional representations of the Arctic and Antarctic. However, it was the Antarctic expeditions, largely happening in the late nineteenth and early twentieth centuries, which displayed the strongest semblances of privation, isolation, and death for the British. During this period, the Empire and its people had begun to doubt the imperial project.[82] Such doubt ushered in a renewed push to prove the heroics of Antarctic explorers like Shackleton and Scott, creating them into imperial heroes by the start of World War I.

In section II, I start with the Empire at its height, during the 1830s to 60s. The section is divided into two parts, the first being an overview of the Sublime and its historical progression from the eighteenth to nineteenth centuries, the second being this esoteric concept's application in polar exploration from the 1830s to 60s. I will examine how the aesthetic principles of this concept, particularly how its dual approach to aesthetics, defined by both wonder and terror, was developed among the English elite as a way of depicting the natural world during the Victorian period. While the Sublime began as a way that philosophers and rhetoricians interpreted literary and artistic works, by the nineteenth century, due to Romantic writers like Byron and Shelly, it had become a norm for explorers and the public alike to depict and understand foreign landscapes as wholly wonderful, terrible, and ultimately Other. The second part of section II will examine the Arctic expeditions of George Back and John Franklin, taking particular focus on how the Sublime was reinterpreted to describe the Canadian North, seeing it as a particularly pristine landscape filled with intrigue and wonder.

Section III will start by primarily focusing on the Arctic and Antarctic landscape as the European world grappled with the early modern period. The section is divided into two parts. The first will examine the literary and artistic reactions to the failed Franklin expedition, taking into account the end of the Romantic Sublime as the English were forced to reconcile with the reality of death and cannibalism in the polar wastes. By looking at the division between the imperial discourse and the way that the poles were depicted by artists and writers like Jules Verne, Edwin Landseer, and Thomas Smith, I show how the North Pole began its transformation from a wondrous to terrible space. Such interpretations of polar space would consequently carry over into Antarctic exploration. The second part of this section will focus primarily on the Antarctic and its association with literary modernism. Due to the increasing body count of polar explorers (and the imperial rhetoric that began to build such men into heroes), literary socialites like T.S. Eliot began to use the poles as catalysts for modern concepts, relating twentieth-century ideas of obscurity, irony, and nihilism through images of polar wastes. Ranging from 1860s to 1920s, this section will ultimately examine the reactionary side of polar discourse, showing how the landscape transitioned from romantically sublime to a space that took on the semblance of the modern world. This literary and artistic reaction consequently created the landscape as a malevolent force, antagonizing it and subsequently shifting Imperial Britain's focus from the landscape itself to the deeds (and deaths) of the explorers themselves.

Section IV of this study will take into account the twentieth-century approach to the Antarctic and its chief explorers. In two parts—the first being about the explorers and their interpretation of the Antarctic, the second examining the public's reaction to these expeditions—I argue that the reimagining of the poles after the Franklin expedition ultimately reconfigured the way that the British interpreted polar exploration. While the English saw John Franklin as a "messenger of daring art," who would bring back his aesthetic reflections of the Canadian North, men like Robert Falcon Scott were nearly worshipped by the British mainland for the mid-Victorian values displayed in his "heroic sacrifice" in the Antarctic. The British ultimately turned the Antarctic explorers and their "white warfare" into national heroes, representing the Empire at its peak in the face of modernism and the First Great War.

Section V will conclude by looking at the polar discourse and its influence on the imperial rhetoric surrounding World War I, particularly in the conception of what was called "The No Man's Land." For soldiers relating experiences of The Great War, the same British depictions of terror and privation associated with the Antarctic worked to provide a language to relate their experiences to the public. Such a space, like the Antarctic, was indescribable in its horror, both compelling those in the trenches to write about it and coming to embody the most gruesome aspects of The First World War.[83] This study ultimately lends insight into the significant connection between polar discourse and World War I discourse, showing how the mythological way of imagining the poles became a catalyst for imagining indescribable spaces of horror during the most destructive war in European history. Like the poles, this way of relating experience could not exist without a literary element. Defined by a specified language of aesthetics and literary representations, the Polar Sublime and spaces like the No Man's Land are part of an alien mentality that only becomes familiar through a broad understanding of cultural history. For contemporary historians, the British fascination with spaces like these, which infuse opposites of terror and mystery, must be situated in both the literary and historical context. The Sublime is a foreign concept, and its Otherness must be explained by exploring the separate philosophical, literary, and historical complexities of British culture during this period of transition.

From the Arctic to the Antarctic, the story of polar explorers, especially those who died on expeditions, was one of sacrifice and duty. The English celebration of these figures and their exploits was brought to a height in the years just before the World War I. Indeed, men like Shackleton and Scott were remembered by the British public as examples of Englishness. They were masculine, they were educated, and above all, they performed their duty "to the last."[84] In a sense, this study shows that two stories happened in the North and South Poles. On one hand, it is a story about how the landscape was perceived and created, moving from wondrous, exotic, and pristine to terrible, desolate, and moribund. On the other, it shows how polar discourse went hand in hand with imperial rhetoric. Explorers were always presented as heroes (some more than others, in Scott's case). In the aesthetic imagining of the poles, there was an opportunity for the British Empire to create a space that reclaimed and proved that the mid-Victorian Britishness of old was still alive and well. Even in its decline, the Empire was able to push forth the idea that modernism, war, and flux would not hold sway over the British spirit itself. And the example of Scott and his contemporaries was the proof needed to keep this artifice in place.

II

During his 1836 HMS *Terror* expedition to the Frozen Strait—a waterway in Nunavut, in the northeastern portion of the Canadian Arctic—British Naval Admiral George Back described to his English readers the jutting ice floes and frozen ocean as "a stranger combination of ruin and confusion with the softness and harmony of the most beautiful tints."[1] He continues to explain the Arctic world as expressing colors of the "faintest emerald" to a deep "cerulean blue," concluding that the picturesque landscape before him "would have been difficult for the most imaginative mind to conceive."[2] In his writings, Back had transformed the frozen north into an "abomination of desolation," holding in its being beauty and ruin and coming to represent the "might of nature" itself.[3] By illustrating these two binaries, the soldier-explorer provided for his readers a prime example of the aesthetic philosophy known as the Sublime—a way of intellectualizing vast landscapes that had developed throughout the previous centuries. This way of interpreting the immense and lofty spaces of the world would ultimately go through many changes throughout the nineteenth century, however, its most basic meaning can be said to embody an infusion of opposites: the beautiful and the awful, the lofty and the terrifying. The Sublime, as related by eighteenth-century philosopher Edmund Burke, "comes upon us in the gloomy forest, and in the howling wilderness, in the form of the lion, the tiger, the panther, or rhinoceros."[4] It is strongly linked to both horror and wonder, working as a kind of window for the observer to gaze upon the dangers and destruction caused by the natural world. While philosophers like Kant and Burke imagined, reimagined, and popularized the Sublime during the enlightenment, the idea found great prominence in Romantic writers, carrying over to the nineteenth- and early twentieth-centuries and becoming a way that many explorers, soldiers, and travel writers chose to relate foreign and non-British landscapes to the English public.

During this period, roughly ranging from the nineteenth to the early twentieth century, many explorers related and *created* foreign, colonial landscapes in such an intellectualized fashion, seeing the spaces they explored as picturesque worlds entirely Other from the Empire's shorelines. The best examples of the Sublime could usually be found in barren, wild, desert, and polar landscapes. The writings of the famous Lawrence of Arabia, like Back, expressed such sublime interpretations. In *The Seven Pillars of Wisdom*, T.E. Lawrence related the Arabian Desert as "inexpressible in words and thought," a space where "emptiness and inevitability thrust upon God as the only refuge and rhythm of being."[5] Key words like "inexpressible" and "emptiness" were used by Lawrence to re-count the experience of a thoroughly non-English landscape like Arabia to the public. Lawrence's writings depicted such landscapes as unknowable and vast, overwhelming to the viewer and forcing upon him a sense of humility in his inability to express them properly through imaginative language. The nineteenth-century writings of explorers and the English public alike abounded with representations of this aesthetic concept. It was a way for the English, both abroad and at home, to interpret landscapes that were non-European, making them seem more familiar, and in a sense taking literary ownership over these vast, indescribable spaces.

While scholars trace the concept of the Sublime throughout British representations of the landscape, it finds its greatest fruition in the polar expeditions to the Arctic and the Antarctic. For instance, Arctic explorer Julius Payer related in The Illustrated London News that such a space was:

A dark sea of open water, dotted with icebergs like so many pearls. Heavy clouds hung in the sky, through which penetrated the glowing rays of the sun, causing the water to sparkle; above was reflected the image of another sun, but of a paler hue. At an apparently immense height the ice-mountains of Crown Prince Rudolf land, bathed in roseate hue, stood out clearly visible through the open mists."[6]

In the above passage, Payer related the vastness of the "dark sea" as a beautiful scene, decorated with sparkling and immense frozen mountains.[7] Such images are characteristic of the Arctic Sublime. In the excerpt, Payer romanticized the landscape in contradictory terms, as both glowing with "rays of sun" and fathomless with dark seas of open water, creating a sense of wonder in its ice-capped majesty. The Sublime, especially in the particular case of these expeditions, became an active way for the English to communicate intellectual superiority in non-English natural landscapes, fashioning a kind of heroic narrative centered on the Empire in the wilderness. To fit into this narrative, the poles, in their vast and unknowable grandeur, were created by both nonfiction and fictional works, manifesting the very principles that defined the Sublime as a normative concept: both representing the violence and terror of pure natural forces and the lofty tranquility of vast mountains and desolate snowy deserts.

Before examining polar exploration and its relation to the Sublime, it is important to look at the aesthetic philosophy itself, in its historical context. While conventionally, the Sublime as an aesthetic concept was manifest in a number of artistic endeavors, ranging anywhere from paintings and poetry, to literature and landscapes, by the nineteenth century, foreign landscapes had become the primary mode of expressing such a form of aesthetics. The Sublime in relation to nature, or the Romantic Sublime, took prominence in the nineteenth century as the push for colonial expansion and New Imperialism set in. The Natural Sublime, as depicted by many English explorers during this period, became the crucial lens through which these men saw and reinterpreted non-English landscapes. The explorers and

English public saw these landscapes as vastly Other and, in a sense, unimaginable. In effect, they used the Sublime to depict such spaces in paradoxical terms: as alien and beautiful, desolate and mysterious, immense and empty. Such an imagining of nature, argued historian Christopher Hitt, is greatly responsible for current depictions of the wilderness, as both a place to find one's self and (at the same time) feel insignificant in the great vastness and unknowability of the Other.[8] While at present, the word "sublime" has lost its previous implications, for ecocritics, literary scholars, cultural historians, and art historians, the term comes with a plethora of meanings, ranging from the emotions that a particular poem or painting can inspire to the intense fear mingled with pleasure that a vast landscape can cause an onlooker to feel.[9] In the framework of this study, the Sublime is used to contextualize Arctic exploration and British imperial culture throughout the nineteenth and early twentieth centuries. It is a concept that goes through much transition, from its early emphasis on wonder to that of terror in later expedition narratives. In effect, the Sublime, as related by British culture, works as yet another tool for historians to trace the Empire's own ideological contention as the Victorian period shifted into a modern period.

While this later aspect of the Sublime was capitalized by explorers to map spaces that the majority of the Empire could not reach, I will argue that its development as a conceptual norm, in both enlightenment and romantic texts, allowed for a kind of European elitist attitude towards spaces like the Arctic and Antarctic, permitting the explorers and the Empire to take control of such spaces on a literary level (if not a physical one). By implication, the recognition of sublime landscapes required educated members of European society, members with "good taste," to articulate properly.[10] In effect, this allowed the Empire to make linguistic claims over spaces. For example, the English public imagined the Arctic as both desolate and beautiful because the English elite interpreted it as such. In the case of the poles, as with others in India or Arabia, native interpretations were considered base and ill-informed.[11] On one hand, the Sublime worked as an epistemological, aesthetic phenomenon, helping the English to talk about non-English landscapes in a way that was commercial and relatable to the public. On the other, it allowed the explorers to domesticate the Otherness that sublime spaces represented, effectively creating a hallowed landscape of the vast and unattainable wilderness. By representing spaces like the Arctic and Antarctic through narratives and fictional reimaginings, the Empire was effectively able to "stage debates about domestic and imperial identities, far from colonial shores."[12] Aside from being a space to prove the worth of Western concepts of masculinity, heroism, and intellectual supremacy, English explorers, alongside the rest of Imperial British culture, were able to create the poles as an ecological phenomenon, set apart from the age of rationalism and industrialization and ultimately becoming as much of an ideology about wilderness as a wilderness itself.

This section is divided into two parts. Part one will examine the historical development of the Sublime as a way that the English talked about foreign landscapes. In effect, its development provided a linguistic tool for the agents of Empire, ultimately allowing explorers like Franklin, Back, Shackleton, Scott, and Mawson to make claims about polar space through their learned understanding of European aesthetic concepts. The historical development of the Sublime into the Romantic Sublime will work as the backdrop for the majority of section one's analysis of polar discourse. This progression, from an esoteric philosophy, used by philosophers to talk about nature through literature and art, to an aesthetic concept, used by explorers when talking about non-English spaces, provides an analytical lens for this study, explaining why the Arctic and Antarctic were expressed by the English in such paradoxical terms. The second part of this section will examine how English writers of fiction and nonfiction manufactured and reimagined the Arctic as sublime, building the foundational conceptions of polar space: as both horrific and beautiful, compelling and desolate. The literary aspect of polar discourse ultimately serves as another point of entry into the historical examination of polar exploration, providing historians with a broader context of the cultural climate of nineteenth-century Europe and how the imperial endeavors of exploration were interpreted by literary socialites who were fascinated by the English push to claim the North Pole.

The use of the word sublime dates to antiquity. In European history, it comes to prominence again during the seventeenth century. During this period, British high society, among other European intellectuals, associated the word with things of literal or symbolic height or vastness, such as mountains or oceans. It was particularly expressed by poets, artists, and authors to exemplify limitless things like God and literary tragedies. As literary scholar Marjorie Nicholson argued:

Awe, compounded of mingled terror and exultation, once reserved for God, passed over in the seventeenth century first to an expanded cosmos, then from the macrocosm to the greatest objects in the geocosm—mountains, ocean, desert The seventeenth century discovered the 'Aesthetics of the infinite'. It was less the metaphysics of infinity that liberated their imagination than an aesthetic implicit in their response to grandeur, vastness, majesty, a gratification of the richness, fullness, vastness of a universe man might not intellectually comprehend, which yet satisfied his unquiet soul.[13]

In the above passage, Nicholson argued that many seventeenth-century Europeans attempted to translate the "transfer [of] the vastness of space into terrestrial grandeur."[14] According to Nicolson, early imaginings of the Sublime, which predated Burke and Kant's philosophical treatise, had already begun to work their way into European public conscious. While European intellectuals associated early seventeenth-century writings about the Sublime more with the infinite rather than nature itself, the concept would undergo a transformation once the late seventeenth-century translation of Longinus' *Peri Hupsous* (translated to *Du Sublime*) was published.

Longinus, a third-century Greek philosopher and rhetorician, wrote *On the Sublime* as a discussion about the effects that great works of literature could have on a viewer. In a translated work, published by French neoclassicist Nicolas Boileau, he argued that such works, like those by the tragedian Sophocles, were hinged upon their ability to create a response in the viewer that was both appalling and compelling.[15] This infusion of conflicting emotions is what the Greek rhetorician called the Sublime. He wrote that the Sublime was a "combination of opposites...inflamed, raving, reasoning, cowering in terror."[16] Such an effect, Longinus argued, was not one of a single emotion or passion, but a "concourse of them all."[17] In this treatise, the Greek rhetorician was looking for the Nature of the Sublime– it was an ontological study. Ontology is the study of being, it is a search for the underling essence of things, whether that be natural or supernatural. In the same way that philosophers like Aristotle were searching for the nature of the plot (the "plotness" of a plot), Longinus' goal was to understand the foundational elements that make up the Sublime, looking for the "Sublimeness" of a particular work of poetry or landscape.

Ultimately, the reemergence of Longinus' work marked the study of the Sublime as a philosophical discipline. English poets and writers interested in this concept were concerned with what made particular works of art and landscapes sublime, shifting the meaning of the term from definitions of the lofty and noble works of art to a more scientifically defined approach – categorized by a rush of emotions brought on by lofty and terrible things like mountains or literary forms of tragedy. Longinus was really concerned with the actual, physical, metaphorical, and linguistic qualities of a sublime poem or landscape. He argued that the Sublime, in both literature and landscapes, caused a kind of catharsis to happen upon the viewer, rushing upon him like light coming out of darkness, "ever shining in front of rhetorical figures, relegating to the shade and as it were hiding away their artificial construction." [18] Such a passage showed the Sublime to be less a rhetorical construct and more like the catharsis of a play, where the onlooker was greatly moved by the climactic image of beauty and despair before him. The same could be said about vast and seemingly infinite landscapes. An ocean or a towering mountain, through the lens of Longinus' sublime, could cause a rush of emotions, overwhelming the viewer with feelings of grandeur, awe, and terror.

For seventeenth- and eighteenth-century readers of this translation, Longinus' sublime had called for a reevaluation of aesthetics. It helped to build philosophical structure for the Sublime. In effect, his work stood as a stepping stone for many eighteenth- and nineteenth-century intellectuals. While English philosophers like Edmund Burke built an entire treaties surrounding his interpretation of Longinus' sublime, English poets praised the Greek rhetorician for his contribution to aesthetics.[19] For example, Alexander Pope, an early eighteenth-century poet, expressed his deep esteem for Longinus' aesthetic treaties in *An Essay on Criticism*, claiming that the philosopher's work "strengthens all his (Longinus') Laws, and Is himself that great Sublime he draws."[20] Such a passage praised Longinus himself as sublime for writing such a treatise. Pope, however, was only the first in a long line of enlightenment thinkers who would follow him during the mid- to late eighteenth century.

Edmund Burke, an eighteenth-century English philosopher, contributed greatly to the construction of the Sublime. His philosophical treaties on aesthetics, titled *A Philosophical Enquiry into the Origin of Our Ideas of the Sublime and Beautiful*, would ultimately serve as a forerunner to the binary depictions of the uncivilized worlds explorers were writing about, further honing the language for them to use when confronting landscapes like the Arctic. In his essays, Burke categorized the Sublime as an aesthetic imagining defied by and associated with supremacy, terror, infinity, and astonishment. This association with "pain and danger" alongside terror called forth feelings in the viewer that were both painful and at once pleasurable.[21] This movement from ontological (looking for the defining aspect of an object) to empirical (looking at how the viewer perceives an object) helped to better provide the English explorers with the vocabulary and knowledge to speak about foreign spaces. If objects were intrinsic in their sublimity, then anyone, including Arctic natives, could speak about these spaces with some level of authority; however, if the interpretation relied on the perceiver, then proper education mattered.

Unlike Longinus, Burke's was an epistemological study, interested less in the objective essence underlying particular works of art and more in how the senses came to know such experiences. While still looking for an objective, universal principle to define this particular form of aesthetics, philosophers like Burke were more concerned with how a viewer perceived the external world around him. Consequently, the senses became the footing on which Burke built his treatise. He begins by defining senses that are universal, like taste. For example, Burke wrote that:

We are satisfied that what appears to be light to one eye, appears light to another; that what seems sweet to one palate, is sweet to another; that what is dark and bitter to this man, is likewise dark and bitter to that; and we conclude in the same manner of great and little, hard and soft, hot and cold, rough and smooth; and indeed of all the natural qualities and affections of bodies.[22]

In the above excerpt, Burke claimed that particular senses, such the taste of sweetness, are universal to all. To disagree, argued Burke, would be in "bad taste."[23] Because the senses were argued to be the "great original of all our ideas," Burke was able to make the same claim in the realms of imagination and judgment.[24] Thus, the philosopher set into motion universal laws for aesthetics according to all five senses. By claiming that aesthetic understandings were universal in the same way, Burke argued that a proper taste for the Sublime and the Beautiful could be understood with an appropriate philosophical upbringing.

After defining taste as universal to human experience, in both the aesthetic and physical sense, Burke then went to examine the differences between the Beautiful and Sublime, claiming that the former was "founded on mere positive pleasure, and excites in the soul that feeling which is called love."[25] Ultimately, it the philosopher understood that the Beautiful was a feminine form of aesthetic taste, inferior to the more masculine Sublime, which was founded more upon judgment and reason. The Sublime, argued Burke, brought forth reason and terror "whilst we contemplate so vast an object," causing us to "shrink into the minuteness of our own nature."[26] Only those with base taste would find such an experience entirely terrible.

Burke's expression of the Sublime was a psychological one, felt primarily when the onlooker experienced both the awe and terror brought on by foreign images of vastness, mountainous terrain, empty deserts, the immensity of God, conflict, and nations in ruin. For the philosopher, the Sublime was the strongest of the emotions that individuals were capable of feeling–it was superior to the beautiful in that it forced its subject to confront his own mortality, and through reason and judgment "rejoice with trembling."[27] The Sublime, as communicated by Burke, could be discovered through all the senses. There was a sublime form of taste, touch, sight, hearing, and smell. While this was closer to what later Victorians would understand as the Romantic Sublime, it was not until the writings of philosophers like Immanuel Kant, and particularly the Romantic writers in the nineteenth century, that the Sublime became exclusively associated with natural landscapes.

While Burke's *Enquiry* introduced epistemological principles to the European vocabulary of aesthetics, Kant's late eighteenth-century philosophical treatise attempted to turn such doctrines into a science. He began by reasserting Burke's arguments that aesthetic judgments signify subjective universalities in the viewer.[28] In his *Critique of Judgment*, both the Beautiful and the Sublime were presented by the philosopher as objective, having nothing to do with the object and all to do with the object as it was perceived by the individual.[29] Kant argued that the concept of the Beautiful was ultimately linked to feeling and imagination, making it feminine and consequently the lesser of the two aesthetic ideologies.[30] The Sublime, which required tense reason and understanding to comprehend, ultimately was attributed by Kant as masculine. In addition, he also divided the Sublime into two categories: the quantitative and the qualitative.[31] The quantitative sublime, or the mathematical sublime, was used to explain aesthetic happenings in nature that brought about in the viewer impressions of excessive force or unimaginable quantification, such as the stars. The qualitative sublime was used to explain natural occurrences that overwhelm the viewer or brought forth feelings of insignificance, such as mountains or vast oceans. Both categories were ultimately linked to nature, in its ability to both terrify and awe. For Kant, the Beautiful caused the viewer to reflect upon passions and emotions derived from a particular experience, causing him to relax in its presence. The Sublime, however, as a higher order of aesthetics, caused the viewer to become tense in fear, overwhelming his imagination and making the experience seemingly inexpressible through language. The Sublime, as explained by Kant, required a maintenance of higher understanding of judgment and reason to comprehend.[32] By admitting the initial experience created an initial experience of displeasure, he argued that the experience (with proper education and taste) became pleasurable when we realized what surrender to it signified–that the experience of the Sublime was the moment when imagination turned to reason.[33] In *The Critique of Judgment*, Kant elaborated on this idea by stating that:

The feeling of the sublime is, therefore, at once a feeling of displeasure, arising from the inadequacy of imagination in the aesthetic estimation of magnitude to attain to its estimation by reason, and a simultaneously awakened pleasure, arising from this very judgment of the inadequacy of the greatest faculty of sense being in accord with the ideas of reason, so far as the effort to attain to these is for us a law, it is, in other words, a law of reason, which goes to make us what we are, that we should esteem as small in comparison with ideas of reason everything which forces is great in nature as an object of sense; and which makes us alive to the feeling of this supersensible side of our being harmonizes with that law.[34]

Kant believed that reason, due to its detachment from subjectivity, could ultimately reveal that to be human was to have a "supersensible" quality. This quality, for Kant, proved the value of human endeavors insomuch that it revealed them to be partly based on some greater harmony with objectivity. Thus, the Sublime, by proving that such supersensible qualities existed in human nature, became associated with the highest form of aesthetics.

Though much of its philosophical spine would fail to survive the transition into the Victorian period, the Sublime, and much of its conceptual foundations, would influence nineteenth-century romantics, becoming a universal aesthetic for the elite and well-educated. English romantic writers would take such an understanding of the Sublime, developed philosophically by Burke and Kant, and apply it directly to the natural world around them, transforming nature into a poetical landscape that hid within it truths that only the well-educated Englishman could unlock.

English Romanticism was an artistic and literary movement, running roughly from the mid-eighteenth century into the nineteenth. Arising partly as a response to the industrial and scientific revolutions, many of the key thinkers during this period were responding to a form of scientific rationalism, a belief system arguing that knowledge and reason should be the basis of society in favor of emotion or religion. Although Romantic writers placed imagination and emotion over reason and judgment, they would also use the Sublime to express divergent imaginings of both art and landscapes. Figures like William Blake, William Wordsworth, Lord Byron, Mary Shelly, and Samuel Coleridge were some of the most notable literary figures during this period, and the Romantic Sublime was echoed throughout their works. Indeed, Shelley's *Frankenstein*, Byron's *Chile Harold's Pilgrimage*, and Wordsworth's *The Prelude* contributed to the discourse about foreign spaces. They presented mountains as vast and compelling and isolated landscapes as pristine and intellectually edifying. Such works of literature became familiarized and popularized in the collective public imagination, providing the English with a linguistic backdrop for later nineteenth-century encounters with foreign landscapes.

Throughout the early nineteenth century, Romantic poets used the Sublime to further categorize and relate the surrounding landscapes. The alpine mountains of Europe became a mark for the kind of romantic empiricism practiced by poets like Byron and Wordsworth. In *Mountain Gloom and Mountain Glory*, Nicolson argued that there was a "fierce pleasure" in that these poets found in the "irregularity of Nature."[35] She continued to say that "these eighteenth-century poets have seemed more interested in the expanded earth than in the extended heavens."[36] An example of this was related by Lord Byron, in a passage from *Chile Harold's Pilgrimage*. Byron, an eighteenth-century poet and leading member of the British Romantic movement, said of his trip to the Alps, that the mountains were "the palaces of Nature, whose vast walls have pinnacled in the clouds over their snowy scalps."[37] He continued by relating that they were like the "throned Eternity in icy halls of cold sublimity…all that expands the spirit, yet appalls [it]." In such a passage, Byron used a paradoxical language to relate his experience in the Alps, depicting them as magnificent in the immensity while at the same time appalling to those who viewed them. In addition to Byron, William Wordsworth, another key

Romantic poet, reflected his accent towards Snowdon Hill, one of the highest points in Wales, as:

A blue chasm; a fracture in the vapour,

A deep and gloomy breathing-place through which

Mounted the roar of waters, torrents, streams

Innumerable, roaring with one voice![38]

This emphasis on the "deep and gloomy" hillside mingled with the "roars of waters, torrents, and streams" paradoxically captured the landscape as sublime in imagination. The poet presented the scene as overwhelming to the senses, its combination of opposites palpable only through the lofty and paradoxical romantic language of this period. Similar to Wordsworth, Percy Shelley, while hiking alongside Chamonix Valley, reflected that:

The everlasting universe of things

Flows through the mind, and rolls its rapid waves,

Now dark--now glittering--now reflecting gloom—

Now lending splendour, where from secret springs

The source of human thought its tribute brings

Of waters--with a sound but half its own, Such as a feeble brook will oft assume,

In the wild woods, among the mountains lone, Where waterfalls around it leap for ever,

Where woods and winds contend, and a vast river Over its rocks ceaselessly bursts and raves.[39]

Percy Shelley's interpretation of the landscape once again echoed the inexpressible experience of the Sublime in nature. By reflecting it as dark, then glittering, then leading to gloom and splendor, the poet related a paradox: a highly romanticized landscape, which emphasized the vastness of an immutable and overpowering natural world. In effect, the Sublime, for late eighteenth- and early nineteenth-century poets was a way to recapture a nature that had been polluted with scientific rationalism. By seeing the mountains as both sites of despair and majesty, men like Byron and Wordsworth were able to turn European landscapes like the Alps into isolated, nonhuman spaces where only empiricism and imagination could convey and reveal the truth about such locales.

While many poets related the English landscape as sublime, Gothic authors like Mary Shelley used far away landscapes, specifically the Arctic, to express similar ideas about the Sublime in nature. For example, in her famous novel, *Frankenstein*, she remarked (through the voice of Victor Frankenstein):

The abrupt sides of vast mountains were before me; the icy wall of the glacier overhung me; a few shattered pines were scattered around; and the solemn silence of this glorious presence-chamber of imperial Nature was broken only by the brawling waves, or the fall of some vast fragment, the thunder sound of the avalanche, or the cracking reverberated along the mountains of the accumulated ice, which, by the silent working of immutable laws, was ever and anon rent and tom, if it had been but a plaything in their hands. These sublime and magnificent scenes afforded me the greatest consolation that I was capable of receiving. They elevated me from all littleness of feeling; and although they did not remove my grief, they subdued and tranquillized it.[40]

In this passage, Shelley's protagonist related his journeys through the Arctic world to his readers. Here, her use of sound (or lack thereof) and the images of "vast mountains" echoed key aspects of the Romantic Sublime seen earlier in Byron and Percy. The landscape Shelley presented was undoubtedly a beautiful and heroic space, defined by danger and the immense power of the natural world.

The Arctic, as characterized by Shelley's novel, represented two things. Firstly, it was a space of retreat and reprieve for the Frankenstein monster. The author uses the monster's journey through the frozen North as a purification process, a place where he can be isolated from mankind, finding a sense of peace in the desolate wastes. Secondly, through Victor Frankenstein, she related the world as illuminated with light and epiphany. "From the midst of darkness, a sudden light broke in upon me," related Victor in his journey through the North Pole. He continued:

A light so brilliant and wondrous, yet so simple that while I became dizzy with immensity of prospect which it illustrated, I was surprised that among so many men of genius, who had directed their inquiries to the same science, that I alone should be reserved to discover so astonishing a secret.[41]

In the passage, Shelley related the newfound understanding and gravity of her protagonist's discovery, his own realization that he had a responsibility to the monster that he had created in the book's early sections. In such an excerpt, the light of the Arctic took on the symbol of enlightenment itself, echoing previous philosophical assertions (from Kant and Burke) that the Sublime would ultimately lead the viewer to reason and understanding.

For Shelley, as with many of her Romantic contemporaries, the Sublime had become many things. Being found in the most desolate or lofty of terrains, by the end of the nineteenth century the Romantic Sublime had taken hold in the collective public imagination. While different variations of the aesthetic concept still lingered in art and literature, the natural world, separate from human influence, was the favored subject of British romantics. Harkening to principals set by Kant and Burke, the Sublime redefined the wilderness as a space for self-purification and enlightenment, turning it into a contested territory where Europeans could seek reprieve from civilized life. Its use in common speech also made such spaces, like the Arctic and Antarctic, zones for man's battle against nature itself.

Many Victorian explorers influenced public imagining of polar landscapes, creating them as sublime worlds where nature was at its purest. The discourse developed around the poles reinforced the growing conception of nature as Other, showing it to be a space set apart from human influence, and idealizing it as something ontologically higher than the worlds of industrialization and human occupation. In effect, it allowed such spaces to become just as much intellectual concepts as existing, physical locations. And most notably, sublime spaces could prove the value of Western ideals, providing a kind of imperial testing grown for expressions of English masculinity, intellectual superiority, and heroism.

The remainder of this section will introduce the Romantic Sublime in the context of Arctic exploration. Briefly, I will examine the imperial rhetoric surrounding both the Back and Franklin expeditions, showing how the excitement surrounding the voyages of these men created a primarily British discourse out of the North Pole. Admiral George Back, as both a British officer and artist, presented both narratives and visual representations of the Arctic, further reinforcing its association with the Romantic Sublime. In his writings and paintings, Back related the Canadian North as a pristine landscape, both wondrous and desolate in its conception. I will then turn to the public excitement surrounding Admiral John Franklin's last expedition to discover the Northwest Passage. At the start of the expedition, the public had imagined the Admiral as a "messenger of daring art," revealing a direct association between the explorers and their ability to relate sublime spaces to the British mainland.

By the early to mid-nineteenth century, many Victorians viewed wild and inhuman landscapes through a sublime lens. The wilderness, as literary scholar and ecocritic William Cronon argued, had become "a landscape where the supernatural lay just beneath the surface."[42] For poets like Wordsworth, sublime spaces were more "supernatural than natural," they:

Inspired more awe and dismay than joy or pleasure. No mere mortal was meant to linger long in such a place, so it was with considerable relief that Wordsworth and his companion made their way back down from the peaks to the sheltering valleys.[43]

In the mind of many Europeans, places like the Poles or Arabian deserts were not meant for humans. They were meant to be seen briefly, working more to test individual character through hardships rather than provide riches or material wealth. Moreover, it was through philosophical doctrines and romantic fiction that Victorians were able to see such spaces as "conquerable" through reason and proper education. Spaces like the polar regions ultimately became a literary endeavor, reflecting themes of British heroism and aesthetic superiority in each explorer's return voyage from the Canadian North. Clements Markham, a nineteenth-century English geographer, Royal Geographical Society secretary, and polar explorer, reflected this excitement well. *In The Lands of Silence: A History of Arctic and Antarctic Exploration*, Markham related tense that:

The Polar regions... [are] of surpassing interest and importance. Here we meet with examples of heroism and devotion which must entrance mankind for all times... thereare dangers to be encountered and difficulties to be overcome which call forth the best qualities of our race.[44]

Markham's reflection lends insight into how the explorers played a key role in the transformation of the Sublime into an imperial endeavor. By turning the Arctic into space that "called forth the best qualities" of the English, the Sublime became the basis for a kind of literary colonial expansion. According to literary scholar Hermann Wittenberg, the discourse surrounding the Sublime, "helped to reconstruct key imperial concerns about masculinity, race and civilizational superiority in terms of aesthetics." [45] Since spaces like the Arctic and Antarctic were uninhabitable, dangerous, and alien to the English in both location and geography, this particular brand of New Imperialism held prominence over many of the motivations surrounding expeditions there. Explorers like Franklin, Back, Shackleton, and Scott saw themselves as men out to once again prove the greatness of their homeland. Through their exploits and aesthetic education, they would be able to turn such unknowable spaces into a primarily British phenomenon, representing mid-Victorianism at its peak. Ultimately, the poles allowed the British to prove the value of intellectual superiority, British heroism, and masculinity.

During the nineteenth century, the polar landscape had become the chief subject of its own literary spectacle: a place that, as George Back remarked, *proved* "the feebleness of man" while at the same time "the triumph of spirit over matter," showing to English readers how such men, even in the face of nature's might, could still stand "unvanquished and undismayed."[46] Back's rhetoric, along with many other explorers, artists, and the educated literary socialites, told little of the actual Arctic as a geographical space. Rather, the British related the Canadian Arctic as discourse, bound by the intellectual language of the Romantic Sublime, a language which they used to create the frozen North as a literary, imaginative phenomenon. As both explorer and artist, George Back and the many polar explorers preceding him, romanticized the frozen parts of the globe into a world that "imagination could scarcely picture," filled with "frost-dazzled" sights and immutable horrors. In doing so, explorers were able to claim a kind of intellectual ownership over such spaces, geographically mapping the North through language rather than cartography.

In 1836, Back, equipped with the Terror, set out for the Canadian North in hopes of charting the Frozen Strait. The Victorian explorer, as mentioned earlier in this section, was no stranger to the Romantic Sublime. This can be seen in both his narratives and art. For example, during his 1830s expedition, he reflected, while exploring the Ross Ice Shelf, that the northern hemisphere "was splendidly illuminated by the extraordinary and beautiful phenomenon" of the Aurora Borealis. He continued to relate the sky and landscape as:

Vividly darting its brilliant coruscations towards the zenith in endless variety, and tinging the ice and snow with its pale and mellow light; the remaining portions of the sky are clear, dark, and unclouded, thickly studded with numberless stars, shining with peculiar lustre, the whole forming a striking and romantic scene, difficult to conceive, and impossible to describe ; the awful grandeur and sublimity of which cannot be contemplated but with the most intense interest and enthusiastic admiration.[47]

Phrases like "zenith in endless variety" and "awful grandeur and sublimity" captured well the English perception of the Romantic Sublime in the Arctic. Back's relation of the North Pole as having "numberless stars" and being "impossible to describe" depicted key qualities of the Sublime. In addition, such phrases lend insight into the British explorer's well founded understanding of aesthetics. The Sublime depicted here both overwhelms and inspires awe. While the true Arctic landscape was not a particularly safe place, the Arctic (as imagined by the British) was presented as brimming with beauty and wonder–a depiction that would eventually fade after the failure of the Franklin expedition.

Back's narratives, however, were also accompanied by visual representations. Presented in figure 1, the painting titled "Coppermine Mouth," depicted the Arctic landscape as nearly civilized. As art historian Stuart Houston related in *Arctic Artist*, the painting sought to "fulfil the seminal dictum of the picturesque—harmony of composition and effect."[48] The original engraving of this watercolor painting was published in 1821, ultimately symbolizing British success in the Canadian North.[49] In it, the British were shown to be successfully enduring (and relaxing) while exploring the mouth of Coppermine River. Such a presentation of the Canadian North was commonplace during this period. While Back was hailed as a national hero by the mainland (he was made Admiral shortly after the success of his 1930s expedition), the landscape he related was the British public's primary interest.

Throughout the nineteenth and early twentieth centuries, soldier-explorers like Back made profound and significant contributions to the way that the Empire and its populaces imagined foreign geographical space as Sublime and heroic. Such sentiments found their way to the public in various forms. For example, Lieutenant James Lockwood, a mid-nineteenth-century Arctic explorer and member of *The Greenly Arctic Expedition*, related to *The Times* that:

The awful panorama of the Arctic which their elevation spread out before them made a profound impression upon the explorers. The exultation which was natural to the achievement which they found they had accomplished was tempered but the reflections inspired by the sublime desolation of that stern and silent coast and the menace of its unbroken solitude. Beyond to the eastward was the interminable defiance of the unexplored coast – black, cold, and repellant. Below them lay the Arctic Ocean, buried beneath frozen chaos. No words can describe the confusion of this sea of ice – the hopelessness asperity of it… It was a wonderful sight, never to be forgotten, and in some degree a realization of the picture that astronomers conjure to themselves when the moon is nearly full and they look down into the great plain which is called the Ocean of Storms, and watch the shadows of sterile and airless peaks follow a slow procession across its silver surface.[50]

Here, the usual depictions of the Romantic Sublime are apparent. There is a level of indescribability related by the explorer in his attempts to capture the Arctic scene for his readers. Terms like black, cold, and repellant are followed by phrases like "wonderful" and "never to be forgotten." These divisions were infused by Lockwood's narrative, making it sublime. In effect, the polar landscape presented by the explorer was defined by conceptualizations of awe alongside beauty and splendor, imagining them as places where the most terrible chasm was also magnificent in its vastness.

Such an enthusiasm for sublime aesthetics was additionally demonstrated in the press coverage of the Northwest Passage voyages, particularly in Rear Admiral John Franklin's nineteenth-century expedition. In 1843, the Royal Navy gave command of ships *Erebus* and *Terror* to John Franklin, a seasoned British explorer and Rear Admiral. His objective was to take a crew of around one hundred and fifty men to complete the charting of the Northwest Passage. The Admiral and his ships were met with great excitement from the Victorian public. In an article titled "Departure of the "Erebus" and "Terror" on the Arctic Expedition," one *Illustrated London News* writer remarked in verse:

A desert waste of water lies before—

Behind, the anxious and hospitable shore,

Which lie a parent bird sees ye depart,

Bold winged messengers of daring Art!

We know the sunshine always 'round your path

Cannot attend; the rain and tempest's wrath

Will be your portion; but our pray'r shall be

You live their fury our right gallantly,

And after years you have perchance to roam

That science crown'd you safely seek your home![51]

The writer's emphasis on "messengers of daring Art" related well how the public saw such explorers. They were not simply looking for a practical passage for Atlantic trade routes— there was a level of understanding that these men would communicate back to Europe tales of English greatness in the face of beautiful and desolate places, where "the rain and tempest's wrath" met them in full force.

In the next section, I will continue following the concept of the Sublime in relation to Arctic and Antarctic explorations during the nineteenth century, tracing the polar landscapes' transition from wondrous to terrible, or Romantic to Modern. Section III begins with failure of the Franklin expedition and the public outrage surrounding it. In addition, it will briefly examine the literary and artistic reactions to the tragedy surrounding John Franklin and his crew members. Such reactions, which also include non-English writers, seemed to suggest a hesitation to praise the English obsession with conquering the North Pole. It is here that a divide seems to form, between the literary culture and the British imperial culture. The Sublime, which had hitherto been a tool of imperial Britain, begins to shape into something that modernist writers like T.S. Eliot would use to examine the irony and futility found in such exploits. Nevertheless, this hesitation and division was met (as seen in the Antarctic expeditions) with an even larger fascination with the frozen spaces and the need to make heroes out of the men who went there.

III

In 1838, American author Edgar Allen Poe wrote the *Narrative of Arthur Gordon Pym of Nantucket*. Argued by literary critic Scott Peeples to be "at once a mock nonfictional exploration narrative, adventure saga, bildungsroman, hoax, largely plagiarized travelogue, and spiritual allegory," the novella traced the exploits of the adolescent, Arthur Gordon Pym, as he was exposed to a series of events (including cannibalism, mutiny, and massacre) that led him to the far southern reaches of the world.[1] At the novella's abrupt end, Pym encountered a momentous "shrouded human figure" with skin that hued the "perfect whiteness of the snow."[2] The text was an obtuse work, told in the traditional narrative style of English expeditions coming from the eighteenth and early nineteenth centuries. Both European and American authors, like Jules Verne, Henry James, and H.P. Lovecraft wrote stories either referencing or in direct response to it. Its representation of the polar landscape, with water reflecting a "milky white" hue and panicles of ice that rolled "silently into the sea from some immense and far-distant rampart in heaven" captured much of the Romantic Sublime seen in earlier expedition texts.[3] However, by the late nineteenth century, such spaces also began to represent terrible things, such as death, cannibalism, or madness. The text in many ways anticipated future representations of Arctic and Antarctic landscapes. It used the Sublime as a catalyst for horror, bringing to mind images of beautiful yet terrifying curtain walls of ice, all the while emphasizing the horrors that such expeditions could encounter.

The horrors that polar landscape could subject to the explorers were relatively new to the English public before the failure of the Franklin expedition. As seen in the previous section, exploration of the Arctic world was met with great enthusiasm, being presented by explorers as an indescribable, wondrous landscape of "awful grandeur and sublimity of which cannot be contemplated but with the most intense interest and enthusiastic admiration."[4] However, by the 1860s, continued reports of cannibalism and starvation surrounding the failed Franklin expedition would ultimately begin to shift the Victorian conception of the poles, turning the emphasis from wonder to that of sublime terror.

This section demonstrates how the polar landscape, first Arctic and then Antarctic, began to shift in its representation of the Sublime. I will first examine the public, artistic, and literary reaction to the failed Franklin expedition. In some ways, the deeply felt failure of this voyage marked the end of the Romantic Sublime. In the case of late nineteenth-century polar exploration, the

Sublime, as an aesthetic concept, would become much more of an antagonistic force, turning the landscape into a horrifying space that only the most heroic individuals could endure. In such a way, the Romantic Sublime becomes the Modern Sublime, representing key themes of literary modernism like obscurity, isolation, and nihilism. This section will show that both English and European intellectuals used the tragedy of the Franklin expedition as a catalyst to bring polar space into a modern context. It focuses heavily on the aesthetic uses of the Arctic and Antarctic, showing how authors and artists alike began to separate themselves from the imperial rhetoric surrounding spaces in favor of using them as images to relate modern concepts. More than ever before, the literary aspect of the polar discourse in this period helps to contextualize the transformation of the Romantic Sublime to the Modern Sublime. As the literary depictions changed, so did the language and sublime representations of explorers. The Antarctic was represented as a "grand terminus" by authors like Lovecraft and Campbell.[5] Simultaneously, explorers like Mawson called the space an "accursed country."[6] This transformation, however, could not be contextualized without the failed Franklin expedition, which had consequently "soured the romance" behind early interpretations of polar exploration.[7]

While Victorians showed a tremendous amount of excitement and optimism at the sendoff of *Erebus* and *Terror*, the harsh reality of such endeavors came at a price. The expedition would end in tragedy. Grossly unprepared for the harsh conditions of the North Pole, reports gathered from Inuit locales concluded that the crew had turned cannibal after losing their ships to the frozen wastes.[8] The same Victorians that saw the expedition off felt the outrage, disappointment, and revulsion that came with the reality that some of their own had met such a grisly, inhumane end.[9] "Not here," wrote the poet Alfred Tennyson years after Franklin's death in 1847. The epigraph, which is located on the admiral's tombstone in Westminster Abbey, continued: "The white North has thy bones; and thou, Heroic Sailor-soul, art passing on thine happier voyage now towards no earthly pole."[10] Tennyson's passionate reaction captured the mood of outrage that pervaded England after the news of Franklin's death. Similarly, English author Charles Dickens echoed such outrage in his letters concerning the Inuit testimonies, discrediting the native reports as false and insulting to English dignity. He wrote:

It is impossible to form an estimate of the character of any race of savages from their deferential behavior to the white man while he is strong. The mistake has been made again and again; and the moment the white man has appeared in the new aspect of being weaker than the savage, the savage has changed and sprung upon him.[11]

Dickens's apparent distrust of Inuit testimonies (and his conception of them as savage and brutish) harkens as far back as sixteenth-century European prejudices. Although published centuries before and not directly related to Dickens' and his own beliefs about Arctic natives, the letters of Dionyse Settle, a sixteenth-century European explorer, show that such conceptions of the Inuit were well

71

into place before the nineteenth century. In his expeditions North with English Captain Martin Frobisher, Settle wrote that the natives of the Arctic were as "barren and unfertile" as the country itself.[12] He continued by remarking that "they [were] rude, and of no capacity to culture the same to any perfection; but are contented by their hunting, fishing, and fowling, with raw flesh and warm blood, to satisfy their greedy paunches, which is their only glory."[13] Both depictions present Artic natives as base, weak, savage, scheming, and ultimately unreliable. In effect, for European explorers, as argued by historian Francis Spufford, "the Eskimos belonged in descriptions of the region, in accounts of its natural history, studies in folk-lore, word-paintings of its scenery. They did not belong in the stories of discovery and achievement."[14] Consequently, the Inuits themselves ultimately either became part of the imaginary narrative conveyed by the explorers or were disregarded by them entirely.

In spite of Dickens' distain for Inuit testimony, the specter of cannibalism hung heavily over the Franklin expedition. While still a point of fascination for both explorers and the British public, the experience of the Sublime in the Polar landscapes changed significantly after the testimony was gradually accepted. While these explorers were "messengers of daring art," the reality of starvation, death, cannibalism, and desolation could not be disassociated from the Artic landscape.[15] Paintings like "Man Proposes, God Disposes," as seen in figure 2, appeared only ten years after reports of the failed enterprise. Seen as "offensive" by the recently widowed

Lady Franklin, Landseer's painting was celebrated by *The Art Journal* as a "tragic grandeur," bringing together a blend of "poetry, pathos, and terror."[16] The painting itself presented a shipwreck in the Arctic landscape. While still showing polar space as sublime, the foreground's depiction of polar bears, one tearing at a Union Jack, the other feasting on the remains of some unfortunate explorer, suggested a more horrific imagining of the Artic, replacing "airless peaks" and "silver surfaces" for a much more pessimistic reality of death and digestion.[17] Another direct depiction of the failed Franklin expedition can be found in the 1895 painting titled "Franklin's Last Expedition," by artist Thomas Smith. As seen in the figure 3, the focus of the painting shifts from the Romantic Sublime to that of failure and death. The painting, which is currently displayed at National Maritime Museum in Greenwich, London, was a brutal piece that drew upon a very different polar reality than Back's earlier paintings. The British explorers were no longer enduring or harmonizing with nature, they were devoured by it.

After the Franklin expedition, fictional imaginings of Arctic explorers seemed to be split between heroes and madmen, success and privation. Such depictions, from both artists and the press, suggested that the Romantic aspect of the Sublime had been lost with Franklin's death. While the later media depictions of Antarctic explorers would be used by the Empire as a rallying cry for heroism, many European artist and authors would also depict such men in an alternative light, dramatizing them as tragic figures who fell victim to either their own obsessions with the polar sublime or the physical landscape itself.

Franklin's failure to find the Northwest Passage was also met by a surplus of literary reimaginings, the most notable being *The Adventures of Captain Hatteras*, by French author Jules Verne. This novel, while still representing the Arctic as sublime, also examined the darker state of exploration in the poles. Though not a traditional historical source, the works of Verne, and figures after him, lend insight to the changing climate after Franklin's death. Prior to these reimaginings of polar exploration, the literary environment nearly matched the enthusiasm for Arctic exploration displayed by both explorers and the press. While still a great interest for many Europeans, the texts following Franklin's death were closer to the paintings previously shown in this section. The Arctic was sublime, but death and privation hung over both the landscape and explorers who went there.

In *The Adventures of Captain Hatteras*, Verne explored the lasting effects of Arctic exploration through his story's protagonist, Captain Hatteras. Working as a comment on the Franklin voyage, the piece touched on themes of insanity, cannibalism, and isolation in the far north. In such literary endeavors, Arctic exploration and its search for the Sublime became coupled with a kind of feverish madness, trading in the romantic enterprise related by earlier explorers for the harsher realization that the quest for the Sublime may bring with it more horrific realities than transcendent ones.

In Verne's *Captain Hatteras*, the title character, a British naval officer named John Hatteras, leads an expedition northward and, after a series of misadventures and mutinies, the finds it a barren land that even "the animals seemed to shun."[18] The skeleton crew returned only to see their captain had gone completely mad, inflicted with what Verne called "polar madness."[19] He was remembered by the English people as a hero "equal to the greatest explorers, the rival of those bold men who sacrifice everything to science."[20] The reality, however, is that Hatteras had gone mad in the polar wastes. In the final passages of the book, Verne wrote:

But the sad victim of a lofty passion lived peacefully at the asylum of Starr Cottage near Liverpool, where the doctor had placed him. His madness was of a gentle kind, but he never spoke, he understood nothing, his power of speech seemed to have gone with his reason. A single feeling seemed to unite him to the outer world, his love for Duke, who was not separated from him…This disease, this "polar madness," pursued its course quietly, presenting no particular symptom, when Dr. Clawbonny, who often visited his poor patient, was struck by his singular manner. The doctor observed carefully this odd mania; he understood the motive of this strange obstinacy; he guessed the reason of this walk always in the same direction, and, so to speak, under the influence of a magnetic force. Captain John Hatteras was always walking towards the North.[21]

In the last passage of his novel, Verne presented his "sad victim of a lofty passion" as a product of the "magnetic" influence of the Arctic. Such a contrast can be seen when looking at earlier depictions by George Back or Shelley, who saw the Arctic as intellectually edifying rather than maddening.[22] While Verne still imagined these spaces as sublime, the Arctic by the latter half of the nineteenth century had also turned into a place of horror, isolation, and madness. This shift in Arctic representation can be seen even in the writings explorers who were still going there. In 1881, Rear Admiral George Melville, a U.S. Navy engineer who had taken similar interest in the North Pole, wrote of his journey that the frozen wastes were a "cold, barren plateau." He continued:

The raging of the wind and the pitiless sea, and the roar of the black water of the bay dashing over the ice-foot, made the lonesome picture look colder and more appalling. Drifts of ice and snow choked the ravines and hollows; but, saving ourselves and the famished, skeleton-like survivors, not a living thing appeared on the whitened landscape.[23]

Though English romantics had honed and developed the language of the Romantic Sublime, contemporary nationalities like the United States seemed to emulate it well. With the image of "black water" pushing its way through "drifts of ice," Melville's image of the Arctic harkened to the sublime terror realized in the writings of philosophers like Burke. However, as the body count and shipwrecks continued to grow, the atmosphere of the Northern world was expressed in a very different tenor, bringing forth images of horror equal to the majesty represented by earlier nineteenth-century British explorers.

Though the tragedy of the Franklin expedition marked the end of the Romantic Sublime, it also allowed for the creation of ample discourse concerning the poles. On one hand, non-English writers and explorers, like Verne and Admiral Melville, interpreted polar exploration in the light of its deadly consequences. On the other, the British Arctic discourse, being greatly influenced by the Sublime, grew into an obsession with heroism and sublimity. As Antarctic expeditions began to take hold of the public's imagination, the fascination with conquering such spaces seemed to only grow at the turn of the century. Between 1897 and 1922, The Royal Geographical society would help fund over ten expeditions to the Antarctic, ushering in a new age of polar heroics. And although many of these ventures ended in failure, the explorers, more than ever, would be remembered by British imperial culture as celebrated heroes of Empire.

In the next portion of this section, I will trace the development of the Sublime in the Antarctic literary and narrative representations, examining how English explorers, like Charles Laseron and American authors like T.S. Eliot, John Marin Leahy, and H.P. Lovecraft came to represent the polar landscape with death, obscurity, and irony in relation to the previous Victorian imaginings of polar space. These works helped to usher in a modernist literary representation of the Sublime, showing how much the polar discourse had shifted from the nineteenth to twentieth centuries.

During this period, which spanned from the late nineteenth to early twentieth-century, anxiety had taken the place of the previous optimism and wonder of the mid-nineteenth century. This can be seen in both fictional and nonfictional depictions of the far south. In effect, writings about the Antarctic were reimagined to fit into the chief themes of literary modernism, ultimately contributing to the emphasis of polar terror started after the failed Franklin expedition. The tragic fate of the Franklin expedition marked a shift in Europe's interpretation of the Romantic Sublime. This shift was realized all the more by the literary culture, which presented the consequences of endeavors like Franklin's through the continued emphasis on the horror in the Antarctic, exchanging, in part, the vitality and romance typically attributed to the poles for peril and desolation.[24]

By the late nineteenth century, the view of polar exploration in the collective mind of the Victorian public had shifted from one of sublime awe and wonder to that of sublime terror.[25] Due to a combination of consistent failures in the North Pole and the shifting social environment of late Victorian England, the way that explorers and the public conceptualized landscapes had changed from a valiant optimism to a reflection of the cultural contention that had arisen in the late nineteenth century. Aesthetic concepts like the Sublime heavily influenced the way that the poles were imagined, however, the focus tended to shift more towards horror, desolation, and obscurity, turning the landscape into a more ghastly doppelganger of the wondrous North Pole. This can be seen in the artistic depictions of polar landscapes after the

Franklin expedition and in both the coverage and narratives surrounding the Antarctic expeditions.

In first part of section III, I explored the gradual transformation of the North Pole, from wonder to the disappointed romanticism that arose from the failed Franklin expedition. The end of the nineteenth century seemed to suggest a split between fictional representation and the way that the Empire responded to the death of its most treasured explorers. This split, between fiction and nonfiction is important because literary modernism in many ways served as a mouthpiece for the modern world, greatly influencing historical representations of events like World War I and the desolation felt by the English during and after it.[26]

The voyages South blurred the line once again, as explorers began relate the Antarctic as a heroic and antagonistic space. "We had discovered an accursed country," wrote Australian explorer Douglas Mawson during one of his Antarctic expeditions.[27] Titles like *The Worst Journey in the World*, written by Apsley Cherry-Garrard, who had accompanied Robert Falcon Scott on his ill-fated voyage, seemed to set the tone for Antarctic expeditions. These explorers, though seeing the Antarctic as more terrible than wonderful, were still (and even more so) remembered and transformed into the very best examples of Britishness that the Empire could offer. The popular narratives of Antarctic exploration, which I will be examining further in section IV, serve to show how the Sublime was used to both create the alien wilderness as a heroic, horrifying, and self-asserting space that worked as a response to the ideological uncertainty arising in England as it shifted from a romantic worldview to a modern one.

Before examining the relationship between polar exploration and modernism it is important to briefly discuss a few key themes and figures that influenced and laid the groundwork for modern thought. As examined in previous sections, Victorian and enlightenment thinkers characterized the world through the lens of reason and imagination. Concepts like justice, beauty, and even the Sublime were discernible with proper philosophical education. For the English, there was a sense of stability in the nineteenth century, fixed in cultural identity, faith, and morality. However, during the latter portions of the Victorian period, concepts like feminism, nihilism, and Darwinism, had taken hold in public discourse, upsetting many of the traditional ideas surrounding Britain's own cultural identity. The modern world had begun to form. Figures like Darwin, Nietzsche, Freud, and Marx had questioned many of the established norms of morality, sexuality, gender, and objectivity. These fathers of modernity had helped to usher in a paradigm shift, questioning the objectivity of traditional values in favor of empirical reality. Even the concept of the Sublime had fallen under direct scrutiny. For example, the German philosopher, Friedrich Nietzsche, in the preface to The Gay Science, attacked the ideology, calling it a mere "theatrical scream of passion."[28] He continued:

How strange to our taste the whole romantic uproar and tumult of the senses has become, which the educated mob loves, and all its aspirations after the sublime, lofty and weird! No, if we convalescents still need art, its another kind of art—mocking, light, fleeting, divinely untroubled, divinely artificial art, like a pure flame, licks into unclouded skies."[29]

The Sublime, as presented by the romantics, would not survive modernist literature. Nietzsche, along with his contemporaries, rejected the defining aspects of the concept, like the lofty and eternal, for the more empirical approach, which would ultimately be categorized (as he puts it) by fleeting, artificial, and mocking things. In a similar vein, this reevaluation of aesthetics can be seen in an 1885 lecture by British-based artist James McNeill Whistler. In the lecture, the artist observed that nature "seldom succeeds in producing a picture."[30] He continued to relate that:

The sun blares, the wind blows from the east, the sky is bereft of cloud, and without, all is of iron. The windows of the Crystal Palace are seen from all points of London. The holiday-maker rejoices in the glorious day, and the painter turns aside to shut his eye. How little this is understood, and how dutifully the causal in Nature is accepted as sublime, may be gathered from unlimited daily produced by a very foolish sunset.[31]

In Whistler's argument, the widespread dialogue of the Romantic Sublime, as understood by the public, had reduced much of art into vulgar depictions of a very uniform and uninteresting nature. Such a reevaluation of the concept challenged much of what the explorers and the Empire had sought to prove in the Arctic. Though Antarctic explorers still presented aspects of the Sublime to the English public, the Romantic Sublime and how the public came to understand the actual Northern landscape became less important to Imperial British culture in the twentieth century. While the explorers continued to envision the Antarctic as a space of horror mingled with moments of wonder, the focus of Britain in this period would be to shift the discourse from the landscape to the heroism (and eventual martyrdom) of the explorers themselves. The leadership of Shackleton, the self-control of Scott, and the unyielding drive of men like Douglas Mawson and Frank Wilde would ultimately replace the obsession with sublime spaces, allowing the Empire to cling to and reassert a number of orthodoxies that were under scrutiny during this period, chiefly those surrounding English manhood, courageousness, and superiority.

The Romantic Sublime, as depicted in the last section, had gone through a significant transformation after the Franklin expedition. The Antarctic voyages, while still emphasized by the explorers as sublime, took on a much more terrifying aspect. Explorers, authors, and artists alike presented the landscape as more terrible and desolate than beautiful. However, it is in literary modernism that the landscape took on a sense of obscurity, unknowability, and even irony. In response to figures like Nietzsche and Whistler, modernist authors like T.S. Eliot reimagined such spaces as vailed, mocking, and unknowable. In addition, another group of American authors, namely those associated with the sci-fi horror magazine: *Weird Tales*, would also influence this new imagining of the Sublime.

Although many of the most notable literary representations of the Antarctic were written by non-English authors, their stories were both centered on English interpretations and narratives, ultimately contributing to the landscape's image as terror stricken and sublime.

The writings of T.S. Eliot, particularly in a draft version of his famous *The Waste Land*, work well as a starting point for the historical analysis of the Modern Sublime. In this unpublished section of the poem, the efforts of English explorers were presented as a kind of tragic satire. The South was represented as a space where lost sailors encounter the horror of unknown regions, ultimately meeting their deaths there. In this draft section, titled "Death by Water," the author relates a story of obscurity and death in the polar wastes. An excerpt reads:

Something which we knew must be a dawn

different darkness, flowed above the clouds,

And dead ahead we saw, where sky and sea should meet,

 A line, a white line, a long white line,

A wall, a barrier, towards which we drove.

My God man there's bears on it.

Not a chance, Home and mother.

Where's a cocktail shaker, Ben, here's plenty of cracked ice.

Remember me.

And if Another knows, I know I know not,

Who only know that there is no more noise now.[32]

The above passage related the Antarctic as a space where sailors and explorers met their death in the southern reaches of the globe. Eliot imagined the space without hope of glory, only knowing "that there is no more noise" for his speaker. In the poem, the sailors jokingly met their deaths at the hands of the "cracked ice" they are driven into. Moments before (in the previous stanza) they were in a nightmarish dream world, mesmerized by three sirens who "sang above the wind" and frightened them "beyond fear" and terrified them "beyond horror."[33] Knowing that the sirens are but an illusion, the sailors awoke to meet their deaths at the great wall of a frozen continent. For Eliot, the polar world was shrouded with obscurity. In his poem, the landscape became a device that ultimately represented the anxieties of modern literary thinkers. It was also used in a mythological sense (as seen by Eliot's placing of the sirens), bringing on themes of discovery, mystery, and death at the hands of the natural world.[34] In addition, by claiming that the sirens were only an illusion, Eliot's verse seems to suggest the ethereal nature of classical values. Ultimately these sailors awoke to the reality that such things would not bring meaning to their deaths, which would only be realized by the ice capped wall into which they crashed.

In addition, some of the best twentieth-. literary examples of Antarctic horror came from various publications in *Weird Tales*, a fantasy and horror pulp magazine started by ex-journalist J. C. Henneberger. These publications, namely Campbell's *Who Goes There?*,

Lovecraft's *At the Mountains of Madness*, and Leahy's *In Amundsen's Ten*, associated science fiction and horror with the Antarctic landscape. Like Shelley's *Frankenstein*, the polar south became a place where creatures dwelled. For example, *In Amundsen's Tent*, written by Martin Leahy, told a story of unnamable horrors discovered by British explorers in the far south. Through the familiar frame narrative, Leahy's short story followed a group of explorers, led by a man called Sutherland, who discover the abandoned tent of the famous Norwegian explorer, Ronald Amundsen. At the heart of the South Pole, the tent was transformed into a site of immutable horror. The team, after searching the areas surrounding the camp, discovered a severed head of a fellow explorer named Robert Drumgold. At first they believe the Norwegians had turned cannibal, but upon further inspection, the narrator remarked that the head had either been "chewed" or "hacked" off from the trunk of the body.[35] It was the creature that they discovered inside the tent, however, that truly defined the scene. Leahy provided no description of the thing in the abandoned tent. It was unknowable, indescribable, and entirely inhuman. When Sutherland looked at the thing, he was petrified by fear and left mute in the presence of it. The passage read:

Sutherland came staggering back and, I believe would

have fallen had we not sprung and caught him.

"What is it" cried Travers. 'In God's name, Sutherland,

What did you see?"

Sutherland beat the side of his head with his hand, and his

look was wild and horrible.

"What is it?" I exclaimed. "What did you see in there?"

"I can't tell you—I can't! Oh, oh, I wish that I had never seen it! Don't look! Boys, don't look, into that tent— unless you are prepared to welcome madness, or worse.... Is this the South Pole? Is this Earth, or are we in a nightmare on some other planet?"[36]

Leahy's association with the indescribable horror discovered in the Antarctic harkens back to key aspects of the Romantic Sublime. However, here, the Sublime had become indescribable in its unworldly awfulness. Unlike the Arctic, the space was not defined by its indescribable mystery and beauty. It was a space that created monsters and nightmares; and to dwell in its snowcapped regions for too long would surely "welcome madness." [37]

Polar madness was also a chief theme in H.P. Lovecraft's novella *At the Mountains of Madness*. In his Antarctic fiction, Lovecraft related the far south as a "bleak realm of ice and death."[38] Throughout the novella, the frozen wastes were presented as a dwelling for evil things. While surveying the Antarctic mountains by plane, Lovecraft's narrator related:

In the whole spectacle there was a persistent, pervasive hint of stupendous secrecy and potential revelation; as if these stark, nightmare spires marked the pylons of a frightful gateway into forbidden spheres of dream, and complex gulfs of remote time, space, and ultra-dimensionality. I could not help feeling that they were evil things— mountains of madness whose father slopes looked out over some accursed ultimate abyss.[39]

For Lovecraft, such a space was a world of ineffable horror and mystery; it held suggestions of "vague beyondness" and called to mind feelings of "utter remoteness, desolation, and aeon."[40] The story itself follows a group of geologists, led by the narrator, William Dyer, as they travel deeper and deeper into the most unknown and ancient mountains of the Antarctic. The climactic ending of the novella set the narrator in direct confrontation with a "shaggoth," which was, like Leahy's creature, defined by being undefinable in its horror. After glancing at the monstrosity pursuing them in the deep recesses of Antarctica's vast mountains, the narrator related:

Unhappy act! Not Orpheus himself, or Lot's wife, paid much more dearly for a backward glance…The words reaching the reader can never even suggest the awfulness of the sight itself.[41]

The shaggoth is later revealed to be an amorphous black, bubbling mass. As Dyer related, it was "something different altogether, and immeasurably more hideous and detestable."[42] Traces of the Antarctic Sublime run throughout Lovecraft's text. The vastness of Antarctica's mountains infused with the inexpressible terrors beneath them were similar to even the Romantic Sublime. However, like Leahy's story, *At the Mountains of Madness* presented a landscape defined by very modern themes. The

Antarctic, as depicted by such literary figures, was imagined as wholly obscure, nihilistic, and terrible.

Such interpretations are literary, of course. However, they work well to add a historical context to the cultural climate of the modern world. Even English explorers imagined the Antarctic as harboring some terrible secret or malevolent force. For example, Charles Laseron, who traveled with Douglas Mawson in his early twentieth-century expeditions to the Antarctic, related that the landscape "'seemed so bleak, so absolutely desolated, so lifeless."[43] He continued:

Later, when sledging over its surface, these characters seemed to merge into a relentless, resentful and definite personality, which ever waited implacably for the single false step that would hand the intruder into its power. One had the impression of fighting, always fighting, a terrible unseen force.[44]

This "terrible unseen force" was made manifest in the fictional writings about the Antarctic. And the image of the Antarctic itself, taking on a "resentful and definite personality," captured well the transformation of the poles from the mid-nineteenth to early twentieth centuries. In effect, as the Sublime and its reinvention drifted further into obscurity, the focus on it had to be reevaluated in the way that the British Empire interpreted the mapping for regions that were understood as sublime. Still armed with the intellectualized language of sublime rhetoric, Antarctic explorers became the central focus of celebration, rather than the landscape. They were out in the polar wastes performing what Shackleton called "white warfare," proving that the Englishness of old still existed in a time that questioned the very identity (and the ability to understand such an identity) of the British people.[45]

This did not change the reality, however, that modernist figures like Eliot still occupied the same elite class as those who clung to traditional conceptions of heroism. Due to the inaccessibility of such spaces and the language needed to talk about them, the poles during the twentieth century were still reserved for those in the elite classes. The political and aesthetic uses of the Antarctic landscape were (as in the nineteenth century) barred by those who had the educational background to talk about it; even if their objectives were divided, the landscape's imagining by British socialites still told the same story of Britishness and its development of an elite, upper class language.

In the section IV, I will examine the polar landscape (and those who went there) in the context of the modern world, exploring how the Empire and the public realigned their focus from landscape to the actual explorers themselves. While still existing among literary critics and artist, the Sublime, as a tool of the Empire, gradually declined in the focus of public discourse, leaving only the story about the explorers and their heroic deaths as the chief topic in pre-world war Europe. As the polar wastes were remanufactured and imagined by artist to represent modernist themes of irony, alienation, and obscurity, the explorers (like Shackleton, Scott, and Franklin) became images that were visited time and again to remind the citizens of the British Empire of their own heroic heritage.

Here, more than ever before, the British mainland celebrated these men as heroes of Empire. These explorers presented the Antarctic, or Modern Sublime as a more dangerous, horrible, and desolate landscape, all the while making their experiences there more heroic. It was their deaths (or rather martyrdom), however, that took on a new meaning for the British in the face of modernity. From Boy Scout teachings to cigarette cards, the image of Scott (in particular) was elevated as a paragon of English heroism and manhood. He, as well as the other Antarctic and Arctic explorers, were seen as exemplar subjects of the best of English virtues: temperance, masculinity, stoicism, selflessness, and self-control. The section will conclude by examining the relation of the polar landscape to English heroism—how it was shaped, reshaped, and ultimately neglected in reaction to the Sublime and its connection to literary modernism.

IV

On March 29th, 1912, just two years before The Great War, Robert Falcon Scott, an Antarctic explorer and English Naval officer, wrote a heartfelt letter to the English people. The letter was written on the eve of his death. It expressed his deep love and gratitude to the nation and ultimately celebrated his own passing in service to it. Scott and his men had become trapped by an Antarctic blizzard and, without proper provisions, had begun to freeze to death. The letter was at once a tragic goodbye and self-assertion of British courage in the face of certain demise. Unsurprisingly, the British mainland greatly mourned his passing. All the while, however, the explorer's valiant death was thereafter used as a rallying cry for the Britishness of old.

In one of the Antarctic explorer's many memorials, English clergyman Canon Rawsley sanctified Scott's polar sacrifice, likening him to a Christian martyr. In order to inspire emulation among his congregation, he wrote that Scott, on the eve of his death was visited in his tent by Christ himself. The poem read:

Christ stood by and pitifully smiled,

Showing the crown of thorns and wounded feet.

But ere the brave heart stiffened into ice

The tent became a palace filled with light

Wherein we met the warriors of the Pole,

Who welcoming cried, 'Lo! life is sacrifice,

Failure so born is victory in the fight,

And true submission manhood's kingliest goal.[1]

Such a passage captured the deep reverence and obsession felt by imperial Britain towards its polar explorers. Rawsley's depiction of the tent becoming "a palace filled with light" even suggests a kind of divine assumption into heaven. In addition, the line "failure so born is victory in the fight" works to set the primary theme of this section. In reality, many explorers died, in both the Arctic and Antarctic. The landscape was harsh and unforgiving, and though Norwegians like Ronald Amundsen were prepared for the severities of the polar world (due to his experiences with the Inuit), many English born expedition leaders refused to practice such methods of survival, favoring starvation rather than adopting Inuit practices. Thus the perspective on such expeditions had to change. In seeing the Arctic and Antarctic as a sublime horror, the English had reimagined the landscape as an antagonistic force. The twentieth-century discursive practices of imperial British culture were more interested in a story of English heroes and their battles with the natural world. While nature won in many accounts, the Empire of the late nineteenth and early twentieth century used this as an opportunity to elevate expedition leaders to national heroes. While many of these men ultimately died, the mid-Victorian values that they represented only needed them to die well, with English dignity and courage.

This predominantly British interpretation of the poles put the actual landscape in a unique and complex position. On one hand, the polar landscape developed further as one of the mouthpieces of modernity, standing as a symbol of Europe's failure to master the world around it and bringing into question the ultimate effectiveness of the Empire and its agents. On the other, the poles, and the accumulated body count of the explorers, were used by the Empire to create a heroic discourse for soldiers and the public in a wartime environment. Scott's death, alongside Shackleton and Franklin's, became a rallying call for the press, inspiring young Englishmen to join the fight and "be British" as the explorers were.[2]

This section has two goals. First I will examine the Antarctic landscape and narratives of its chief explorers, showing how such a practice of aesthetics further emphasized such spaces as terrible, masculine, and heroic. Through the narratives of men like Ernest Shackleton, Douglas Mawson, Frank Wilde, and Robert Falcon Scott, the further development of polar landscapes shift between unimaginable horror and mysterious beauty. While this exists in retellings of the Arctic, the emphasis on terror in the Antarctic, as shown in section III, is much more apparent. Secondly, I will show how the representation and fascination with the Antarctic gradually became secondary in favor of seeing those who went (and died) there as national heroes. These men, particularly Robert Falcon Scott, became a rallying cry for the Empire in the face of the modern world. They came to represent the Victorian values that were under scrutiny, "proving" that such concepts existed if one was willing to die for them.

While the obsession with polar explorers was very real in the nineteenth century, the Antarctic explorers became the primary symbol and focus of the expeditions, rather than the landscape. Though these expeditions operated under the guise of scientific discovery, the majority of them were seen as races to the pole, the last unconquered territory for the Empire. These men knew that they were seen by much of the public as English heroes. And the Sublime language they used was ultimately a catalyst for Imperial propaganda. If the Antarctic was indeed as horrible and, as Mawson said, "an accursed country," then those few and brave English men who traveled there were all the more heroic for doing so.[3] Through the writings of both the Antarctic explorers and the British mainland, these explorers were able to show that pre-modern, traditional imperial values still had worth. In effect, Antarctic explorers, like Shackleton, Wilde, Mawson, and Scott, through their letters and narratives, created in the South Pole a geographical space that responded to the twentieth-century debates concerning English masculinity, heroism, and superiority. The Antarctic, through the imagining of the Sublime, was made to "prove" the masculinity, endurance, and intellectual supremacy of the English, turning it as much into an imperial space as an imagined wilderness filled with both compelling beauty and terror.

This change in polar exploration, the gradual association with the poles as a place of horror and (very) possible death, ushered in a new way of seeing the white capped landscapes. While the aesthetic fascination, the scientific curiosity, and the desire for new frontiers was a point of public interest for many English during this period, the effects of discursive practices surrounding the Antarctic expeditions can be seen in a broader historical context as imperial endeavors. To such an effect, the English mainland saw explorers during this period as ideal examples of the Empire; in their courage to go against the might and horrors of nature, they were national heroes as much as "messengers of daring art."[4]

Historians recognize the Heroic Age of Antarctic exploration as the later portion of nineteenth-century exploration to the First World War.[5] This period of exploration represented a shift, in both public attention and the motives of the explorers, who had become more interested in a patriotic, personal, and imperial endeavor.[6] It should come as no surprise then that even the expedition names during this "heroic age" reflected such imagery. With titles like *Nimrod*, *Quest*, *Discovery*, and *Endurance*, these expeditions served to set the stage for an attempt made by the Empire to reclaim the traditional values that were gradually declining from the collective conscious of the Victorian public.[7] The South Pole was the last space in the world that was unmapped, and the greatest desire of many good Englishmen was to carve into the white landscape an image of their national pride, personal achievements, and aesthetic reflections.[8] Even more so than in Arctic expeditions, the Sublime and its rhetorical usage was a way to talk about the landscape on European, imperial terms, experiencing it through contested concepts of masculinity and heroism.

This repurposing of polar exploration came with grave consequences for the explorers themselves, however. The Heroic Age of Antarctic Exploration saw the celebration and, sadly, the martyrdom of many European explorers. Men like Ernest Shackleton, Robert Falcon Scott, and Ronald Amundsen all died while venturing South.[9] At the peak of their careers, these men worked together and against each other in hopes of being the first to conquer the last spaces of the globe. *The Times*, which (along with the *Illustrated London News*)[10] had always been a great supporter of polar exploration, celebrated Shackleton and Scott as "glorious gentlemen heroes" and "the embodiment of the virtues of the age."[11] During this period, Shackleton managed to travel farthest South, coming short only ninety-seven miles of his goal to be the first to the pole,[12] while Scott and Amundsen became the first to reach the South Pole itself (Amundsen being the winner of the two). Such feats, as told by the explorers who performed them, were heroic achievements that added to foundations of both scientific and geographical knowledge.

Frank Wild and Shackleton, alongside men like Douglas Mawson and Robert Falcon Scott, played key roles in the contribution of imperial discourse concerning the South Pole. As the Victorian authors and Arctic explorers before them, these men described for the Victorian public a Polar landscape filled with conflicting beauty, turning the frozen wastes into a geographically imagined landscape that was both entirely compelling and treacherous.[13] Shackleton, during the *Nimrod* expedition, reflected poetically that Mount Erebus was "grim, rugged, gloomy and grand," a place that was "proud, unconquered and unyielding."[14] While men like Shackleton did not use the term "sublime" in their relation of the Antarctic to the public, the nineteenth-century understanding of the word fits his relation of the mountain. Shackleton offered an imagining of Erebus that was conflicted by portraying the volcano as both compelling and uninviting. The romanticizing and personifying of the polar landscape pervaded his memoirs, letters, and journal entries, adding to the already vibrant discourse that reinforced this image of the Antarctic as more dangerous and unforgiving than its northern double. In such a context, the Sublime had become a vision of nature that was treacherous and antagonistic, making the task all the more challenging and the rewards for any Englishman who could survive it all the grander.

This shift, from the Romantic Sublime to sublime terror can be seen even more so in Shackleton's later expeditions. During his *Endurance* expedition, Shackleton, while gazing out into the frozen waters surrounding Antarctica, related his surroundings as a "beautiful and lonely prison."[15] At the time, ice floes had trapped the ship and its crew, imprisoning them near the Antarctic continent.[16] Shackleton's description of the landscape conveyed a melancholy mood consistent with his previous reflections. The explorer understood the beauty as mingled with a kind of desolate bleakness, thus transforming the frozen wasteland into an imagined, unforgiving landscape. This desolation and bleakness reflects well the change that was happening in the late Victorian period, more in line with modernist authors like T.S. Eliot than their romantic predecessors like Shelly or Byron. The Sublime, while still a major tool used to interpret alien landscapes, had changed in consequence to the continual failures and deaths that defined such expeditions.

Australian explorer Douglas Mawson, in accordance with Shackleton's representation of Antarctic melancholy, related an additionally terrible side of the polar landscape to the Victorian public. Mawson reflected Antarctica as being "on the fringe of an unspanned continent, where the chill breath of a vast, polar wilderness, quickening to the rushing might of eternal blizzards, surged to the northern seas."[17] The explorer's reflection of the polar wilderness was a powerful representation of what he called the accursed "home of the blizzard."[18] A particular journal entry, concerning his arrival at Aurora Peak, captured the blend of terror and wonderment that defined the twentieth-century understanding of the Sublime.[19] In the passage, Mawson related:

When the sun's disc emerged into the rift there was light; but dim, cold and fleeting. The smallest irregularity on the surface threw a shadow hundreds of yards long. The plain around was a bluish-grey chequer-board of light and shade; ahead, sharp and clear against the leaden sky, stood the beautiful Aurora Peak, swathed in lustrous fold—the chariot of the goddess herself. The aweful splendor of the scene tended to depress one and make the task more trying. I had never felt more nervous than I did in that ghostly light in the tense silence, surrounded by the hidden horror of fathomless depths.[20]

Here, Mawson's understanding of the Antarctic landscape works as a key example of how the English explorers, through their narratives and perceptions, created the Antarctic as Sublime, harkening back to earlier nineteenth-century imaginings of it. By seeing the peak as both fathomless and splendid, Mawson defined the spatial landscape of the South Pole in strong contrasts, adding further to this conception of the Antarctic as a sublime place of harsh divisions and dangers, a landscape unsafe and unfit for any but the strongest of wills and men. "We had pierced the veneer of outside things," wrote Shackleton in his 1913 journey south, continuing:

We had suffered, starved and triumphed, groveled down yet grasped at glory, grown bigger in the bigness of the whole. We had seen God in His splendours, heard the text that Nature renders. We had reached the naked soul of man.[21]

The landscape was presented by these men as filled with danger, suffering and rapture, rewarding only the boldest and courageous of men with striking images of beauty and glory.

The Antarctic's association with Victorian manhood was another predominantly mid-Victorian attribute given to it by the explorers who went there. Due to the rise of the "new woman," the Antarctic ultimately became one of the spaces used to battle against modern conceptions of gender. There was a strong push in the late nineteenth and early twentieth century to reclaim and prove the heroic worth of masculinity and heroism. Such concepts were tied together for the Empire. An example of this can be seen in Royal Geographical Society's President Leonard Darwin luncheon speech. On the eve of the Terra Nova's departure, Darwin declared that "they [Scott and his men] mean to do or die – that is the spirit in which they are going to the Antarctic."[22] He continued:

Captain Scott is going to prove once again that the manhood of the nation is not dead, and that the characteristics of our ancestors, who won this great empire, still flourish amongst us; and although we, who stay at home, have no right to share in a particle of the glory, yet the self-respect of the whole nation is certainly increased by such adventure as this.[23]

The RGS president's claim that Scott would show "once again that the manhood of the nation is not dead" captured both the connection to and the push for the kind of resurgence of heroic masculinity happening in response to modernity. The Empire believed that such endeavors as Scott's, who would "do or die" out in the Antarctic, would recapture such concepts from the contested territory they had fallen into. In a period that saw the rise of the "masculine novel," the imperial culture of Britain ultimately used such approaches to heroism to further define gender lines and roles, keeping women from exploring such locations.[24]

In effect, the absence of women from this discourse contributed greatly to its creation of the Antarctic space as masculine, allowing late Victorian conceptions of manhood to contribute to the British explorers' geographical interpretation of space in the Polar Regions. In the same way that these spaces became Anglicized through continual British representations, they also became a space associated proving manhood. In the understanding of the explorers who went there, the Antarctic required an active, physical state to endure.

Mawson, affirmed this in his correspondences with Paquita Delprat, his fiancé. "This everlasting silence is unbearable," wrote Paquita to Mawson in October of 1913. She continued:

I don't want to doubt you my dear but I'm afraid of the fascination of the South. All the members say they would go again and here is Shackleton off again. Will a calm life ever satisfy you? I have seen unhappiness where I thought all was well. Calm homes also have skeletons in a cupboard it seems. I want you to reassure me that all will go well with us and our love.[25]

The correspondences between Mawson and his fiancé stand as one of the many cases of female exclusion from the mapping of the polar continents. Unsurprisingly then, it is not until after the 'Heroic Age' of Antarctic exploration that we see any female polar explorers. In consequence, this absence allowed for a masculine gendering of the geographical space by making it a kind of "no man's land" for men only. Mawson reinforced this gendered understanding to his fiancé, telling her:

It so happens that man is a combination of certain qualities—woman of others. There is a fundamental dissimilarity just as surely as there is a similarity. In the biologists classification, the female represents the passive vegetative state—the male is the active animal state. This generalization is true of woman and man no matter how much the *new woman* may think to the contrary.[26]

Such an attitude toward both women and men existed among many of the English explorers during the period. Victorians understood spaces such as Antarctica as wild and adventurous, and thus masculine. "Freedom of the coming work is the knowledge that it is in a *man's* work," wrote Shackleton to his wife, Emily, during the *Nimrod* expedition.[27] Here, Shackleton is explaining the daily complications and delights that follow one another during an expedition. In such an understanding, these efforts were entirely expected to be principally suited for men.

In one particular case concerning applications for the *Endurance* expedition in 1914, a group of three women hoping to gain admittance onto the voyage had contacted Frank Wild, who oversaw the applications.[28] To the disappointment of the women, Wild sent a letter of rejection stating conclusively:

Sir Ernest Shackleton begs to thank Miss Peggy Pegrine, Miss Valerie Davey and Miss Betty Webster, for their letter but regrets there are no vacancies for the opposite sex on the Expedition.[29]

Similarly, Mawson, when organizing his own expedition in 1929, was approach by twenty-five female applicants who were "attracted by the novelty of adventure." [30] Mawson, like Shackleton, denied all female admittance, claiming that "the coming expedition was unsuitable for women."[31] Such cases showed the extent of female exclusion from polar exploration. While the expedition leaders excluded a number of capable female scientist from the poles, women like Emily Shackleton continuously awaited the return of her husband, who had, in such a period, effectively fled from domesticity and embraced the new masculinity that was on the rise.[32]

Masculinity in the late nineteenth century was a changing concept, ultimately becoming less domestic as the turn of the new century approached.[33] Due to the rise of the "new woman," the growing popularity of men's adventure novels, and the call for a New Imperialism, men like Shackleton, who had a family perpetually waiting for his return, sought to live out this new manliness through the separation and adventure provided by his journeys south.[34] What some historians call "the flight from domesticity"[35] shifted the traditional Victorian understandings of masculinity—that of the domestic head of house—to a manhood that imitated what Author Conan Doyle called the "modern masculine novel."[36] These men, who often romanticized about the manly accounts of life presented in travel narratives and adventure novels, had only a thin line dividing the world presented by such "masculine novels" of the time and from the world of Britain's Empire.[37] While on the *Endurance* expedition of 1914, Shackleton described the seemingly conflicted and gendered pulls that this "flight from domesticity" had on Victorian men:

Last night, before we sailed, I wrote to Emily. I tried to explain that when I am there my heart is half-here, facing the cold spray and the ice. And, of course, when I am here, some part of my heart is there. Sometimes, I think I am no good at anything but being away in the wilds just with men. The South marks us, makes us unfit to live in civilization. The longing to return is our blessing and our curse.[38]

The explorer, in his reflections, drew a relation between the Antarctic and the new shape of masculinity. The Antarctic, for these men, became a space of escape and isolation from women. It was a place of comradery, a male-only sphere that shaped the way that the rest of Victorian England related to Polar Regions, ultimately reflecting greater trends of masculinity in the late nineteenth century.[39] These masculine assertions, along with their often fatal consequences, worked in concordance with explorers' imaginings of the Polar Sublime to turn the Poles into an entirely British landscape.

In contrast to the masculine Antarctic, the expeditions lead by American female explorers, particularly through the writings of Mina Hubbard, reflect the Empire's original aim in the poles: to create a picturesque, aesthetic mapping of the wild, uninhabitable spaces of the globe. Though

British women were largely bared from polar exploration during this period, there are a number of accounts where American women explored unmapped regions of the globe. Particularly, the expeditions Harriet Chalmers Adams and Mina Hubbard provide insight into the female experience in foreign landscapes, challenging that Mawson's earlier assumption that such expeditions were ultimately "unsuitable for women." For example, Adams, who had over twenty of her travel stories published in The *National Geographic* magazine, wrote:

I've wondered why men have so absolutely monopolized the field of exploration. Why did women never go to the Arctic, try for one pole or the other, or invade Africa, Tibet, or unknown wildernesses? I've never found my sex a hinderment; never faced a difficulty which a woman, as well as a man, could not surmount; never felt a fear of danger; never lacked courage to protect myself. I've been in tight places and have seen harrowing things.[40]

Indeed, Adam's life was a testament for the capability of women in the context of exploration. Throughout her years in South America, the explorer traveled over 100,000 miles of wild terrain. [41]

In addition, Mina Hubbard's expedition narratives reflected a very similar form of aesthetic mapping as nineteenth-century figures like George Back. In 1905, Hubbard set out to complete the unfinished mapping, from the North West Rive to the Ungava Bay, of the eastern Canadian landscape known as Labrador.[42] Years earlier, in 1903, her late husband, Leonidas Hubbard, had failed in his Canadian expedition, mistaking a small river for the

Naskaupi River.[43] After backtracking his journey for nearly two months, Leonidas died in the Canadian wilderness, starving due to the arrival of winter.[44] Determined to finish her husband's work, Hubbard set out to map the Labrador wilderness. Her narratives relate the landscape as beautifully sublime. However, unlike Mawson and Shackleton's twentieth-century relation of the concept, the American explorer's language drew more on earlier nineteenth-century imaginings, seeing the Labrador Mountains as "magnificent in all directions."[45] Indeed, Hubbard's narratives read like a painting of the picturesque. In one passage she related that a small lake, near Hades Hill, was:

Black as ink now under leaden sky and shadowing hills. The lake, which was three-quarters of a mile wide, dipped not only with the course of the river but appeared to dip also from one side to the other. Not a ripple or touch of white could be seen anywhere. All seemed motionless as if an unseen hand had touched and stilled it. A death-like quiet reigned and as we glided smoothly down with the tide we could see around us a soft, boiling motion at the surface of this black flood, which gave a sense of treachery as well as mystery. As I looked down the long slope where the river appeared to lose itself into the side of the mountain it seemed to me that there, if anywhere, the prophecy of Job's dream must be fulfilled. Cerberus might easily be waiting for us there. He would have scarcely time to fawn upon us till we should go shooting past him into the Pit.[46]

The Sublime, as discussed in section II, is apparent here. Hubbard's infusion of both mystery and treachery, tranquil stillness and inky black water, created a scene of both serene beauty and underlying terror. Throughout her writings, words like mysterious, grand, beautiful, and glorious were used to describe the wild landscape.[47] Indeed, such reflections stood in stark contrast to the contemporary writings of twentieth-century Imperial British explorers. They were, more concerned with the aesthetic space than conceptions of imperial pride or manhood. And in many ways, Hubbard herself proved to be just as suitable a "messenger of daring art" as British explorers like Back or Franklin.

In the end, the explorers' depiction of the poles as both sublime, heroic, and masculine helped to define them as exemplary heroes. And when they died on expeditions South, the English public mourned them in the same way that they would any public idols, by remembering them as martyrs. Originally stated by sixteenth-century explorer Sir Humphrey Gilbert, Robert Falcon Scott wrote:

He is not worthy to live at all, who, for fear and danger of death shunneth his country's service or his own honour, since death is inevitable and the fame and virtue immortal.[48]

Scott, an officer in the Royal Navy and renowned Polar explorer, was a suitable subject for English patriotism. When the relief party discovered his body, along with those of his men, frozen and lifeless in the South Pole, the public lamented once again in bitter outrage.[49] Like Franklin before him, Scott became an English martyr.[50] His death, along with the death of Shackleton, turned him into an even larger hero to the Victorian home front. When the relief team found Scott's frozen encampment, it also discovered a farewell letter from the explorer to the English people among the bodies. Scott, satisfied to die as a proper Englishman, told his fellow countrymen:

I do not regret this journey, which has shown that Englishmen can endure hardship, help one another, and, meet death with as great a fortitude as ever in the past. We took risks—we know, we took them. Things have come out against us, and therefore we have no cause for complaint, but bow now to Providence, determined to do our best to the last.[51]

Scott described the Antarctic as a catalyst for the exercise of bold heroics, permitting him to publicize his "splendid failure" with great, and ultimately English, dignity. The explorer's final reflections did much to reveal how he understood England's place in relation to Antarctica. The white landscape was a place for he and his crew to prove their masculinity, their bravery, and live (or die) in a fashion that they interpreted as thoroughly English. Indeed, Scott confirmed this understanding of the polar region to J.M. Barrie, the Scottish author and dramatist best known for his creation of Peter Pan, Scott, telling his friend, for the last time:

We are pegging out in a very comfortless spot. Hoping this letter may be found and sent to you, I write a word of farewell.... More practically I want you to help my widow and my boy—your godson. We are showing that Englishmen can still die with bold spirit, fighting it out to the end. It will be known that we have accomplished our object in reaching the Pole, and that we have done everything possible, even to sacrificing ourselves in order to save sick companions. I think this makes an example for Englishmen of the future, and the country ought to help those who are left behind to morn us. Goodbye. I am not at all afraid of the end, but sad to miss many a humble pleasure which I had planned for the future on our long marches. I may not have proved a great explorer, but we have done the greatest march ever made and come very near to success. Goodbye, my dear friend.[52]

In his final moments, Scott represented himself, and his followers, as a proper Englishmen. By showing that "Englishmen can still die with bold spirit," the explorer, in dying in the frozen wastes confirmed the seeming relation between the Poles and English heroism by reinforcing the association between the landscape and the Empire.[53]

The remainder of this work will explore the cultural obsession with men like Scott, Shackleton, and Franklin, taking particular emphasis how Scott's death and letters became a rallying cry from the old to the young during a pre-world war environment. The *Daily Mail* and *Daily Chronicles* contributed greatly to this heroic discourse; the former asserting that Scott's "English heroism has given to the world yet another epic." [54] In Scott's death, the Empire had the tools needed to prove the great value in the heroic struggles of Englishmen in the Antarctic. The landscape and its terrible sublime had molded the greatest of men who would ultimately set an example for a nation at the brink of war.

The reaction to Scott's death in 1912, only two years before the First Great War, was met with cultural obsession. His suffering and heroic sacrifice was amplified and marketed throughout the Empire. One *Daily Graphic* writer wrote that he was 'more like an ancient Greek than a modern naval captain."[55] The same year, *The Times* celebrated Scott's final message in verse, claiming that: "Every man who aspires to play a man's part, and every boy who would be a man' to take Scott's words to heart."[56] It is here that these concepts, the making of the Antarctic as heroic and masculine, the imagining of the polar landscapes as Sublime, peaked in popularity, being used as imperial propaganda and transforming the polar discourse itself as a bedding for wartime rhetoric.

One example of this kind of excitement about the explorers and their heroic examples can be seen in the encouragement of Britain's youth to be British as these men were British. "Let us tell the children how Englishmen can die," as one writer of the *London Evening News* put it, became the slogan of the times.[57] Another example can be seen in the final lines of the publication *Scott's Message to England*. Published only months after the captain's death, the short pamphlet was made to chronicle the exploits of the soldier turned martyr. It ends with the somewhat cryptic sentence: "The nation's loss is also the nation's splendid gain. The bones of heroes are also the glorious seeds of heroes to come." [58] There is a strong relation here between masculinity, heroism, and sacrifice that captures well the political environment of twentieth-century imperial British culture. In effect, proper English manhood meant the ability and discipline to perform heroic acts of national duty. As presented by both Scott and the press, the explorer performed such duty by dying for England and proving that such British forms of heroics still existed.

Such heroics were largely reactionary in their attempt to rekindle the English peoples' belief in the traditional Victorian values explored earlier in this paper. In addition, this attempt to "tell the children how Englishmen can die" works in accordance with the recent creation of the Boy Scouts Association.[59] And after Scott's death, there was an even further push for scouts to emulate such Edwardian heroics. The characteristics of the movement, expressed through comradery, national duty, and discipline, was fit firmly alongside the stories of Antarctic exploration. Founded by Robert Baden-Powell, the Boy Scouts of

Britain's empire were encouraged by newspapers, scoutmasters, and Powell alike to think of Scott as an ideal example of what the organization stood for. As related in the memorial of Sea Scout Witt and Scoutmaster Carnall, Powell referred to the dead men as "brave companions" who showed that "boys can die like men in carrying out their orders calmly in the face of danger."[60] The scoutmaster then drew connections between the scouts and men like Scott, claiming that the polar explorer "died proving himself one of the most energetic Scouts of our nation."[61]

Powell was not the only Englishman to draw the connection between polar explorers and the nation's youth. In a 1913 *Daily Mail* publication, titled "Well Done," a young girl named Mary Steel wrote a short poem in dedication to the Antarctic explorers. It read:

Though nought but a simple cross,

 Now marks those heroes' grave,

Their names will live forever!

Oh England! Land of the Brave![62]

Less than a year before World War I, there was a stronger push than ever to the youth of Britain with the polar explorers who died in the South. Another example of this can be seen in the opening of *How Five Brave Englishmen Died*, a memorial story for the Scott expedition written by folklorist Arthur Machen. The opening line to Machen's text read:

Children: You are going to hear the true story of five of the bravest and best men who have ever lived on the earth since the world began. You are English boys and girls, and you must often have heard England spoken of as the greatest country in the world, or perhaps you have been told that the British Empire ... is the greatest Empire that the world has ever seen ... when we say that England is great we are not thinking of the size of the country or of the number of people who live in it. We are thinking of much more important things, and if you listen to the story that is to be read to you, you will find out what greatness really does mean.[63]

Machen finished his story by stating that:

These brave men died; and now you know what we mean when we say that they were great. They feared no danger, they never complained, they did their very best, each one was willing to give up his life for the others, and when they knew that there was no hope for them they laid down their lives bravely and calmly like true Christian gentlemen.[64]

This concept of teaching the youth "what greatness really does mean" was used time and time again years later during The Great War. Indeed, the line between war rhetoric and polar discourse had been blurred by propaganda posters that stated "the Empire needs men" and "helped by the young lions, the old lion defies its foes." In 1914, at Scott's memorial service and statue unveiling, the prime minister reflected of Scott that "there is no figure of our time who holds and will retain the same enduring place in admiration and gratitude of his countrymen."[65] Scott and his contemporary explorers were ultimately an example for England in the face of Modernism and War. They were seen as "true Christian gentlemen" and proof that, as Markham put it, "the spirit which influenced the patriotic adventurers of the Elizabethan age was still alive."[66]

Even with their graves in the Arctic and Antarctic, these men and their association with the Poles and empire seemed only to increase. In 1866, the nation dedicated statues to Sir John Franklin and the men lost on the *Erebus* and *Terror*. Upon the dedication day, "bystanders cheered," reported the *Times* and "a group, including some ladies, looked from the balconies with indescribable emotions."[67] The Victorian public memorialized Franklin for his bravery in the North while Scott's expeditions South christened him a glorious gentleman hero who fully embodied the virtues of the Empire. Obituaries similarly memorialized Shackleton, who had died during the *Quest* expedition. In 1922, the New Zealand Merchant Service Guild organized a memorial service in honor of Shackleton. The surviving members of the *Quest* expedition buried his body on the small island of South Georgia, the "gate of the Antarctic," with "his head pointed towards the South that he so well loved."[68] One *Times* article related that:

While his body rested "in an ice-bound land," Shackleton was also "here, at the heart of the Empire, in the church which may be said to have been re-dedicated to our greatest man of action, his name and his daring and his achievement were honored by those best acquainted with their full significance.[69]

Shackleton's burial position, pointing southward, only served to reinforce the link of these explorers to the landscape, further bringing imperial significance to their quests. A month after news of Shackleton's death, C.P. Conigrave, an Australian journalist for the *Northern Territory Times and Gazette* told his readers:

I believe that as long as there is a spiritual meaning to this life of ours, the world will be a better place for having known such brave and gallant men, the recital of whose deeds gives an added tingle to one's blood. Shackleton had many a time looked death squarely in the face without fear, and it somehow seems, despite the pity of it all, peculiarly fitting that his last conscious thoughts were associated with the league-long rollers that sweep towards the Great White South, the romance and mystery and fascination of which fashioned and shaped his whole life.[70]

Conigrave's obituary presented the romanticism associated with these men. His own remembrance of Shackleton ultimately reflected how the vast majority of the British public remembered its dead explorers: as heroes of the Empire. Franklin, Scott, and Shackleton all died while attempting to conquer the frozen wastes, leaving an English mark on the white landscape. While their tombs were ice-bound in the frozen world that they loved, their homes were in the Empire. They carved into the Great White South a space for Englishness, exclusive to men and filled with the "mystery which still hovers over those far-off seas of ice and remote bays."[71]

The First Great War marked the end of the Heroic Age of Antarctic Exploration, and with it, English exploration in the poles. While the expeditions to the Polar Regions were less consequential for other people, in a sense, due to their extreme locations, the death of nearly all the leading explorers proved that nature was the victor over British endurance. However, the English polar explorers had transformed the white spaces of the Arctic and Antarctic into the sublime, masculine, and imperial images for the Victorian imagination.[72] The Victorian notion of the Sublime found importance in the way that it worked through much of the literature, art, and personal narratives of the time, creating a vivid imagining of the Polar

Regions in both the armchair adventurer and the actual explorers. Such a notion, in its drive to discover perilous beauty, coincided with a new-adventure driven masculinity that kept men like Shackleton and Mawson returning repeatedly to Antarctica. These men, being influenced by aesthetics, masculinity, and the world of Empire, were connected to the frozen world through the romanticism they created, becoming heroes in a growing tradition of imperial martyrs, transforming these spaces into Imperial landscapes. While men like Scott, Franklin, and Shackleton Combine into one footnote at the end ultimately failed in their intent to reach and survive the Poles, they were still remembered and celebrated by the English as heroes of the Empire.[73] "To reach the Pole is an aim of pure idealism" wrote the *Daily Mirror*. It continued:

It is not besmirched by the dusty finger of politics. The explorers who have lost their lives in the pursuit of this ideal had no hopes of planting prosperous colonies upon the frozen surface of the Pole. There is no wealth to beckon them thither... The sacrifice of our heroes is unsullied and unstained.

In such a passage, English press coverage, as many times before, echoed the romantic notion that the polar explorers were the best of Britishness. In the face of world war and modernist philosophies, they reminded the youth of Britain to "play the man" and "be British" as these men were.

From John Franklin to Ernest Shackleton, the English celebrated these men as national heroes, even in their failures. Joseph Conrad referred to such men as "the great knights-errant of the sea," pursuing the "grails" that rested at each end of the world.[74] For Conrad, they were national and imperial figures, spreading Englishness across the world's oceans. In contrast, H.P. Lovecraft, who was writing short stories directly following the "heroic age" of Antarctic exploration, fixated his attention on world they inhabited. The early twentieth-century author depicted the Antarctic as a "bleak and blackish" landscape with nightmarish spires that broke into half-luminous clouds, gazing down from ice-coated slopes into an "accursed and fathomless abyss."[75] Due to the influence of the polar explorers, Lovecraft, among others, viewed the arctic as a space that held within it reminders of "utter remoteness, separateness, desolation, and aeon."[76] The English explorers who related these depictions of the Sublime, manliness, and Englishness, shaped an imagining of the Polar landscapes through their odysseys that held considerable influence during and beyond Victorianism. Men like Shackleton, Scott, and Mawson had inexorably become a part of a tradition that molded the way in which their contemporaries and predecessors understood foreign landscapes—for better or worse—and the people who could (or could not) inhabit them.

V

On August 1st 1914, Shackleton set out with a crew of twenty-eight men on the Imperial Trans-Antarctic Expedition. Being that Scott and the Amundsen had already made it to the South Pole, the expedition's goal was to have British explorers cross the entire southernmost continent. While docked at Margate two days after setting off from London, Shackleton discovered that England had called for naval mobilization. The Great War had begun. The explorer eagerly volunteered the use of the *Endurance* and its crew for the coming battles with Germany and Austria-Hungary, to which the admiralty, with orders directly from Winston Churchill, promptly replied: "Proceed."[1] The *Endurance* sailed onward from Margate to the Antarctic, sporting a union flag and with the renewed blessing from King George himself.[2]

When Shackleton left London at the dawn of World War I, he left a decorated hero of the Heroic Age of Antarctic Exploration. The *Daily Mirror* had previously hailed the explorer's ventures to the Antarctic as a "British triumph."[3] This expedition however, would ultimately be the last in the Heroic Age. The war, which was expected to last only a few months, carried on for over four years. After yet another failed voyage in the Antarctic, Shackleton would not return to the same heroic optimism that had encouraged the *Endurance* to "proceed." The explorer and his men returned to a Europe that was tearing itself apart.

Throughout this study I have explored the transformation of the Sublime in relation to polar landscapes. In doing so, I divided the poles into two phases: the Romantic and the Modern. The first section focused primarily on the Romantic Sublime, its conception as an aesthetic philosophy and its later transformation into a way that Romantic poets, authors, and the Victorian elite came to understand vast and untamable natural spaces. From philosophers like Kant and Burke to Romantics like Byron, Shelley, and Wordsworth, the Sublime was fashioned throughout the eighteenth- to mid-nineteenth century as a way to see and categorize landscapes, presenting to the British public non-English spaces that were pristine and wondrous in their intellectual conception. In addition, section II looked at how figures like George Back, who was both an arctic explorer and established painter, applied the Sublime to both his Northern expedition narratives and paintings. This optimistic imagining of the Canadian North would change, however, with the failure of the Franklin expedition, which made up the first half of section III.

The third section of this study explored the conceptual transformation of the Sublime during a period of Victorian anxiety and disappointment. It was not the failure of the Franklin expedition that caused such outrage amongst the British public so much as the way that the men were reported to have died. Franklin and his crew had supposedly turned cannibal and the image of it haunted the British for the remainder of polar exploration. In almost direct response, the literary environment surrounding polar exploration shifted in its thematic depiction. While the Arctic in the early nineteenth century was understood as representing intellectual enlightenment and indescribable wonder, by the 1860s it had become associated with themes of madness, death, and obscurity.

Such interpretations would be even further realized in the period known as the Heroic Age of Antarctic exploration. While still imagined as sublime, the Antarctic became a much more antagonistic landscape, representing for the British some of the key themes of modernism, namely obscurity and nihilism. In order to subvert this, the focus shifted much more to the explorers and their achievements as British heroes. Men like Shackleton and Scott came to represent ideal examples of mid-Victorian values, conveying through their actions qualities of stoicism, national duty, and heroic endurance. These men were remembered for their "white warfare" against a natural environment. Only the best examples of British manliness could endure such a landscape. Indeed, endurance was key for Antarctic explorers who were elevated to heroes of Empire. Throughout the Great War, Imperial Britain did not need survivors, so much as young men who were willing to endure hardships and perform their duty "to the last."[4]

The final section of this study will discuss polar exploration's influence and role in The Great War. The themes that defined the British experience in the poles, particularly those of sublime terror in the Antarctic, can be seen throughout the discourse surrounding the war. Like polar exploration, the ways that soldiers in the trenches of France and Belgium documented their experiences were largely literary in their implementation. British soldiers fighting in trench warfare created myths, wrote poetry, and told stories about the horrors on the Western front.[5] While polar discourse was not solely responsible for this, it worked as a testing ground, in part, creating the kind of language and literary interpretation that would represent the British experience during the First World War. This can be seen in the depictions of the "No Man's Land," which was traditionally understood as the war-torn battlefield between two opposing trenches.[6] Such a space was metaphorical as well as literal. It could represent a space of peace, providing a safe zone for soldiers to retrieve their dead without fear of being attacked by opposing factions.[7] On the other hand, it could also provide the most gruesome images surrounding The Great War. As historian Fran Brearton wrote, in *The Great War in Irish Poetry*, the No Man's Land was often defined by "men drowning in shell-holes already filled with decaying flesh, wounded men, beyond help from behind the wire, dying over a number of days, their cries audible, and often unbearable to those in the trenches; sappers buried alive beneath its surface."[8] She then related that such a space was "beyond language" and "description."[9]

Like the Arctic and Antarctic, the landscape between armies became a nearly indescribable space of desolation and emptiness. In it, soldiers heroically died for their country, mythologized the war, and came face to face with the modern world.[10] Spaces like the No Man's Land had both the lure and horror of twentieth-century sublime landscapes. While polar failure may have been a foreshadowing of the Empire's inevitable decline, World War I, which was approached with the same optimistic spirit as the expeditions North and South, would prove that such an inevitability was already well on its way.[11]

Although The Great War marked the end of the Heroic Age of Antarctic Exploration, the polar discourse, in both its sublime and heroic qualities, can be seen throughout representations of the battlefields and trenches on the Western front. Indeed, even without the Antarctic as a literary vessel, the heroic mythologizing of people and spaces explored throughout this study were continued in the representations of The Great War. In many ways, World War I historical and literary representations overlap.[12] While there are a number of reasons for this, the strongest being that Britain's educational system was "conceived on largely humanistic terms," I will argue that polar discourse, with its literary imagining of sublime space and mythologizing of heroes, served as ample ground to significantly influence what would become the key literary representations of the First World War.[13]

In a now famous work in cultural history, *The Great War in Modern Memory*, cultural and literary historian Paul Fussell argued that a great deal of the Frist World War's British representation came from "the literary means by which it has been remembered, conventionalized, and mythologized."[14] This could also be said of polar exploration. Indeed, Francis Spufford, in *I May Be Some Time: Ice and the English Imagination*, claimed that there was a literary imagination driving English expeditions in the poles. A history of these spaces, wrote Spufford, is "an intangible history of assumptions, responses to landscape, cultural fascinations, [and] aesthetic attractions to the cold regions." [15] Both polar and World War I discourse overlap in this area. Each historical period, as understood and presented by the British, was tied to concepts of sublime interpretations of heroism and terror.

Such an influence, namely that of late nineteenth- and early twentieth-century interpretations of the poles, can be seen in the English reflections of battlefields in France and Belgium. The depictions of the trenches call forth images of sublime terror. As such, they became a point of both fascination and horror for those who experienced them. For example, in his memories about life along the trenches west of Hebuterne and Fonquevillers, British Army Officer Charles Carrington reflected:

In fifty years I have never been able to rid myself of the obsession with No Man's Land and the unknown world beyond it. This side of our wire everything is familiar and every man a friend; over there, beyond the wire, is the unknown, the uncanny." [16]

Here, the fascination with "unknown world" beyond the No Man's Land harkens to the same language used to represent spaces in the Antarctic. Like Mawson's reflection of Aurora Peak, which was related as being an "aweful splendor...surrounded by the hidden horror of fathomless depths," Carrington was both obsessed with and horrified by the space between trenches. Indeed, the sharp division of the landscape, of familiar and unfamiliar, known and unknown, reflects aspects of the Sublime as mentioned throughout this study.[17] The landscape during World War I, like the polar sublime, was about strong contrasts and the fascination with spaces that represented them. Myth making also played a substantial role in the No Man's Land. Much like the horror stories that followed the cannibalism associated with the Franklin expedition, this space came with its own grotesque (and very similar) tale of human failure.

As the twentieth century progressed, the poles became more and more associated with horror, or monstrosities. For example, Campbell's *Who Goes There?* introduced a creature that could perfectly replicate anything that it was able to digest, causing mass paranoia among the cast of the novella. In a similar vein, Poe's nineteenth-century story of polar exploration, *The Narrative of Arthur Gordon Pym*, ended abruptly, with the protagonist coming face to face with a towering unknown entity clad in white. Throughout polar representation, there is a sense of the unknown portrayed, whether it be through physical monsters or some mysterious disappearance or death, such as the Franklin incident. This practice was also incorporated into the mythologies surrounding the No Man's Land. Like the poles, the space became associated with mystery mingled terror. Such mystery was usually realized in folkloric depictions of creatures roaming battlefields at night, feeding off of the corpses of unfortunate soldiers. In his 1920s memoir, titled *The Squadroon*, British officer and war correspondent Ardern Beaman reflected upon stories of ghoul-like soldiers roaming the empty battlefield. He wrote:

The Golgotha was peopled with wild men, British, French, Austrian, German deserters, who lived there underground, like ghouls among the moldering dead, and who came out at night to plunder and kill.[18]

Another British officer, Osbert Sitwell, reflected such men as living "in caves and grottos under certain parts of the front line." He continued:

They would issue forth, it was said, from their secret lairs, after each of the interminable checkmate battles, to rob the dying of their few possessions.... Were these bearded figures, shambling in rags and patched uniforms ... were they a myth created by suffering among the wounded, as a result of pain, privation, and exposure, or did they exist? It is difficult to tell. At any rate, the story was widely believed among the troops, who maintained that the General Staff could find no way of dealing with these bandits until the war was over, and that in the end they had to be gassed.[19]

Such stories of cannibalism and madness fit firmly into the twentieth-century depictions of the Antarctic landscape.

Like polar space, the mystery surrounding the No Man's Land was used as a catalyst for horror, producing vivid images of cannibalism, privation, and death. While the location was vastly different, the representation of it was the same. The trench landscape became a wasteland and the British heroes who fought there were swallowed by it. Wilfred Owen, an English poet and soldier, wrote that the snow ridden whiteness of No Man's Land was "like the face of the moon, chaotic, crater-ridden, uninhabitable, awful, the abode of madness."[20] Once again, the wilderness had won out. However, by the end of The Great War, the Empire would not fully recover. While figures like Scott could be used to further inspire would be imperial heroes, the aftermath of World War I was too substantial. And this time, the English public, like Beamon, Carrington, and Owen, would remember the war as a Golgotha of human suffering and demise.

This entire study tells two interwoven histories—the first being an examination of the Sublime and its relation to polar landscapes, the second being about the British imperial culture during a state of anxiety, flux, and ultimately, decline. The importance of polar discourse was hinged upon its relation to Britain and the modern world. The Sublime and its influence on the way that both the European and American elites saw polar wilderness ultimately lends insight to the Empire's struggle with modern challenges. These challenges, from the rise of feminism to the doubt cast over traditional Victorian moral teachings, threw into flux norms of imperial culture. And both polar exploration and The Great War sought to reestablish those norms in the attempt to prove and reestablish English dignity, heroism, intellectual superiority, and endurance. In both cases, this attempt was a colossal failure. The Franklin expedition ended in cannibalism, both Shackleton and Scott died while exploring Antarctica, and The Great War only served to reaffirm the horrors of the modern world. A host of literary representations followed, mocking the attempts of Englishmen as they sought to prove their own conceptions of heroism. Indeed, among all these, the great irony behind the Empire's attempts to avoid the onslaught of decline was its contribution to it. Through its continual attempts to prove that Britishness would not be shaken by the modern world, it became instrumental in its creation.

FIGURES

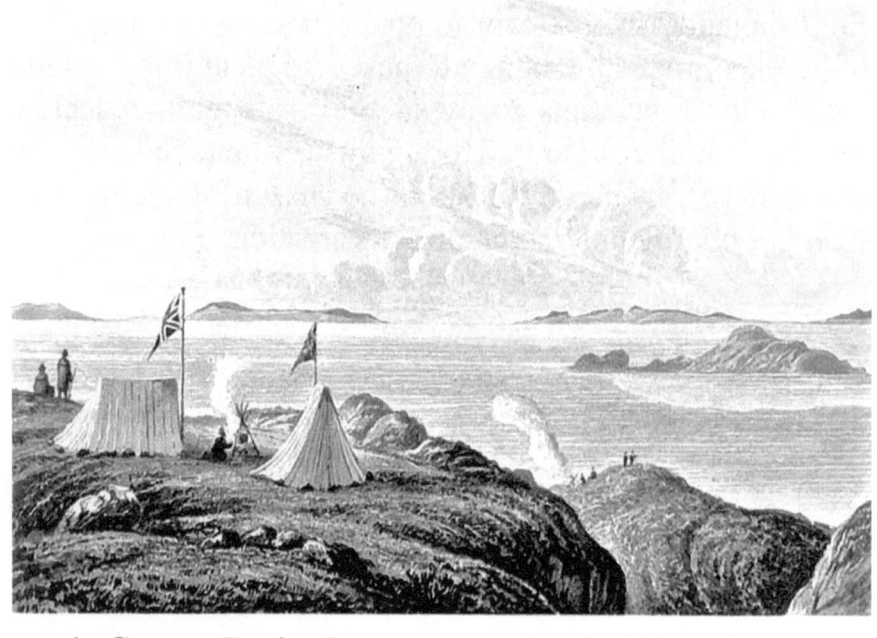

1: George Back, *Coppermine Mouth*, 1821, Watercolor on canvas, Library and Archives Canada, W.H. Coverdale Collection of Canadiana.

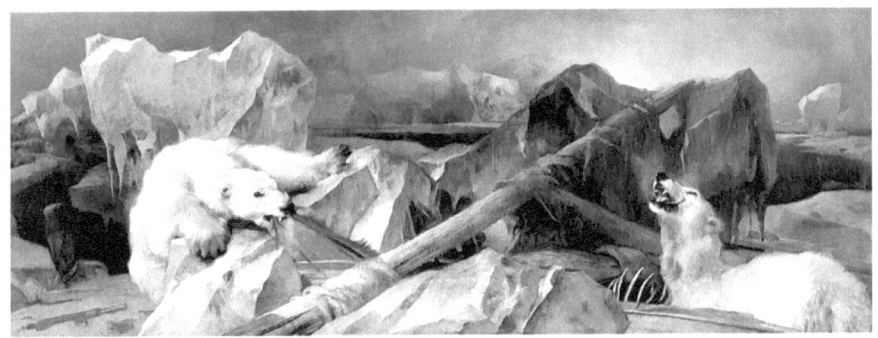

2: Edwin Landseer, *Man Proposes, God Disposes*, 1864. Oil on canvas, Royal Holloway College, University of London.

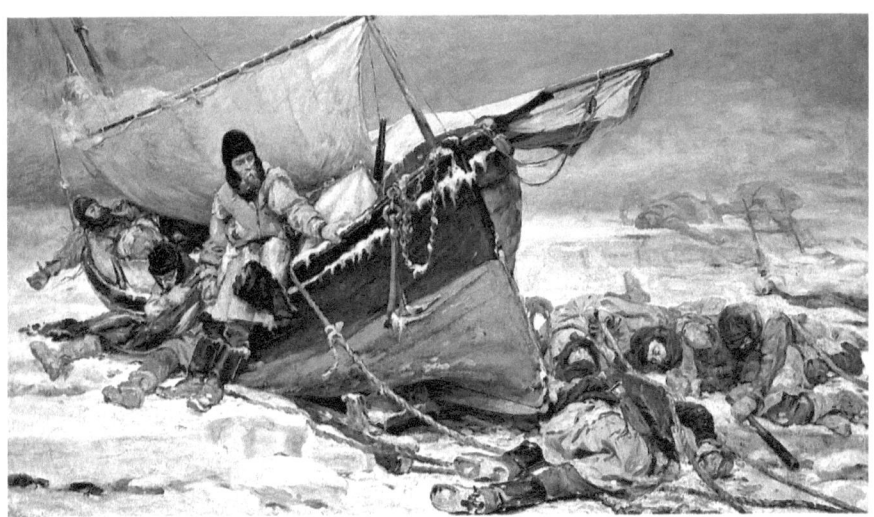

3: Thomas Smith, *Franklin's Last Expedition*, 1864. Oil on canvas, National Maritime Museum, Greenwich, London.

NOTES

I

1. "The Thing, Horror, and Science Fiction," *New York Times*, June 25, 1982, 1.

2. "The Return of the Thing that Stalked the Thirties," *The Times*, August 20, 1982, 6.

3. "The Thing, Horror, and Science Fiction," 1.

4. Elena Glasberg, *Antarctica as Cultural Critique: The Gendered Politics of Scientific Exploration and Climate Change* (New York: Palgrave Macmillan, 2012), 66.

5. Ibid.

6. Bill Lancaster, *The Thing, 1981 Screenplay by Bill Lancaster* (University Reprint, 2012), 114.

7. "A Monstrous Conception," *The Times*, August 25, 1982.

8. John Campbell, *Who Goes There?* (Somerset: Rocket Ride Books, 2009), 3.

9. Ibid.

10. William James Mills, *Exploring Polar Frontiers: A Historical Encyclopedia, Volume 1* (Oxford: ABC-Clio, 2003), 483.

11. Chauncey C. Loomis, "The Arctic Sublime," in *Nature and the Victorian Imagination*, ed. U. C. Knoepflmacher (Berkeley: University of California Press, 1977), 95.

12. John Barrow, "Sir John Franklin's Expedition," *The American Review: A Whig Journal of Politics, Literature, Art, and Science*, Volumes 11-12 (New York: Wiley and Putnam, 1850), 594.

13. Sara Wheeler, *The Magnetic North: Notes from the Arctic Circle* (New York: Farrar, Strauss and Giroux, 2011), 256.

14. Robert G. David, *The Arctic in the British Imagination*, 1818-1914 (Manchester: Manchester University Press, 2000), xvii.

15. Janice Cavell, *Tracing the Connected Narrative: Arctic Exploration in British Print Culture, 1818-1860* (Toronto: University of Toronto Press, 2008), 29.

16. Ibid., 9.

17. "Second Leader," *Illustrated London News*, October 1, 1859, 316.

18. Stephanie L. Barczewski, *Antarctic Destinies: Scott, Shackleton and the Changing Face of Heroism*, (New York: Continuum, 2008), xii.

19. Ibid., 65.

20. Ibid., 299.

21. Mary Shelley, *Frankenstein, or The Modern Prometheus* (Lancaster: Sovereign, 2012), 76.

22. George Back. *Narrative of an Expedition in HMS Terror: Undertaken with a View to Geographic Discovery on the Arctic Shores, 1836-7* (New York: Cambridge University Press, 2013), 189.

23. Piers Brendon, *The Decline and Fall of the British Empire, 1781-1997* (New York: Alfred A. Knopf, 2008), 77; Edward J Larson, *An Empire of Ice: Scott, Shackleton, and the Heroic Age of Antarctic Science* (New Haven: Yale University Press, 2011), 143.

24. "Departure of the "Erebus" and "Terror" on the Arctic Expedition," *London News*, May 19, 1845, 6; "Antarctic Disaster: Loss of Captain Scott and His Party," *The Times*, February 11, 1913.

25. Paul Fussell, *The Great War in Modern Memory* (Oxford University Press, 1975), 1.

26. I. S. MacLaren, "From Exploration to Publication: The Evolution of a 19th-Century Arctic Narrative" *Arctic*, Vol. 47, No. 1 (1994): 50.

27. Ibid.

28. Ibid.

29. Ernest Shackleton, *South: The Endurance Expedition* (New York: Signet, 1999), 1.

30. Edward J. Larson, An Empire of Ice: Scott, Shackleton, and the Heroic age of Antarctic science (New Haven: Yale University Press, 2011), 289-90.

31. Timothy Parsons, *The British Imperial Century, 1815-1914: A World History Perspective* (Lanham, Md.: Rowman & Littlefield, 1999), 4-5.

32. Ibid., 21.

33. Ibid., 21.

34. Geoffrey Barraclough, *An Introduction to Contemporary History* (New York: Basic Books, 1965), 56.

35. Brendon, *The Decline and Fall of the British Empire*, 12.

36. Ibid., 168.

37. Larson, *An Empire of Ice*, 144.

38. Niall Ferguson, *Empire: The Rise and Demise of the British World Order and the Lessons for Global Power* (New York: Basic Books, 2003), 202.

39. Ibid., 202.

40. Elleke Boehmer, *Empire Writing: An Anthology of Colonial Literature, 1870-1918* (New York: Oxford University Press, 1998), 277.

41. Parsons, *The British Imperial Century*, 3.

42. Ibid., 21.

43. Larson, *An Empire of Ice*, 35.

44. Charles Kingsley, *The Works of Charles Kingsley* (Philadelphia: John D. Morris & Co., 1899), 213.

45. John M. MacKenzie, *Imperialism and Popular Culture* (Manchester, UK; Dover, N.H., 1986), 3.

46. Ibid.

47. George Orwell. *A Collection of Essays* (New York: Mariner Books, 1970), 118; Rudyard Kipling, *Rudyard Kipling: Poems* (New York: Everyman's Library, 2007), 96.

48. Arthur Penrhyn Stanley, *The Life and Correspondence of Thomas Arnold*, Volume 2 (New York: Philadelphia, G.S. Appleton), 398.

49. Kingsley, *The Works of Charles Kingsley*, 213.

50. MacKenzie, *Imperialism and Popular Culture*, 266.

51. Ibid., 7.

52. Dane Kennedy, *Britain and Empire, 1880-1945* (Harlow : Longman, 2002), 28.

53. Ibid., 28-2.

54. Ibid., 29.

55. "Speech to the Cobden Club Denouncing the Brussels Sugar Convention," *The Times*, November 29 1902, 12.

56. Emily Hobhouse and Ruth Fry, *Emily Hobhouse: A Memoir* (London: J. Cape, 1929), 109.

57. Jennifer Hobhouse Balme and Emily Hobhouse, *To Love One's Enemies: The Work and Life of Emily Hobhouse Compiled from Letters and Writings, Newspaper Cuttings and Official Documents* (Cobble Hill, Canada: Hobhouse Trust, 1994), 121.

58. John Gooch, *The Boer War: Direction, Experience and Image* (Portland: Frank Cass, 2000), 102.

59. Gooch, The Boer War, 11.

60. "South-African War Mortality," *The Parliamentary Debates: Fourth Series, Second Season of the Twenty-Seventh Parliament if the United Kingdom of Great Britain and Ireland* (Fetter Lane, London: Wyman and Sons, 1901), 583.

61. Dane Kennedy, "British Exploration in the Nineteenth Century: A Historiographical Survey," *History Compass* 5, no. 6 (2007): 1879.

62. Fussell, *The Great War in Modern Memory*, 12.

63. I. S. MacLaren, "The Aesthetic Map of the North, 1845-1859," *Arctic Institute of North America* Vol. 38, No. 2 (1985): 101.

64. Ibid., 101-102.

65. Michael Krans, "Writing For an Elsewhere: Author(ity) and Authenticity in the Texts of the First Franklin Expedition (1819-1822)," *Studies in Canadian Literature*, Vol. 24, No. 1 (1999): 9.

66. Ibid.

67. James Marlow, "English Cannibalism: Dickens after 1859," *Studies in English Literature, 1500-1900*, Vol. 23, No. 4 (1983): 652.

68. Ibid., 653.

69. Jeremy W. Crampton and Michel Foucault, *Space, Knowledge and Power: Foucault and Geography* (Burlington, VT: Ashgate, 2007), 177.

70. Edward W. Said, *Orientalism* (New York: Vintage, 1979), 71.

71. Felix Driver, *Geography Militant: Cultures of Exploration and Empire* (New York: Blackwell Publishers, 2001), 43.

72. Matthew H. Edney, *Mapping an Empire: the Geographical Construction of British India, 1765-1843* (Chicago: University Of Chicago Press, 1999), 32.

73. Edney, *Mapping an Empire*, 32.

74. Paul Carter, *The Road to Botany Bay: An Exploration of Landscape and History* (New York: Knopf, 1988), 36.

75. Ibid.

76. Linda Colley, *Britons: Forging the Nation, 1707-1837* (New Haven: Yale University Press, 1992), 361.

77. Kathleen Wilson, *The Island Race: Englishness, Empire, and Gender in the Eighteenth Century* (New York: Routledge, 2003), ix.

78. Ibid.

79. Ibid., 168.

80. Ibid., 4.

81. Wilson, *The Island Race*, 4.

82. Brendon, *The Decline and Fall of the British Empire*, 159.

83. Fussell, *The Great War in Modern Memory*, 119.

84. "Antarctic Disaster: Loss of Captain Scott and His Party," *The Times*, February 11, 1913.

II

1. Back, *Narrative of an Expedition in HMS Terror*, 189.

2. Ibid.

3. Ibid., 190.

4. Edmund Burke, *A Philosophical Enquiry into the Origin of Our Ideas of the Sublime and Beautiful* (London: Routledge and Paul, 1958), 114.

5. T.E. Lawrence, *Seven Pillars of Wisdom* (Hertfordshire: Wordsworth Editions Ltd., 1997), 41.

6. "Cape of Pillars, Prince Rudolf Land," *The Illustrated London News*, September 11, 1875, 6.

7.. Ibid.

8. Christopher Hitt, "Toward an Ecological Sublime," *New Literary History*, Vol. 30, No. 3 (1999), 606.

9. Loomis, "The Arctic Sublime," 97.

10. Burke, *A Philosophical Enquiry into the Origin of Our Ideas of the Sublime and Beautiful*, 33.

11. Edney, *Mapping an Empire*, 32.

12. Hill, *White Horizon*, 3.

13 Marjorie Nicolson, *Mountain Gloom and Mountain Glory; the Development of the Aesthetics of the Infinite* (Ithaca, NY: Cornell UP, 1959), 143.

14 Ibid., 273.

15 Paul Crowther, *The Kantian Sublime: From Morality to Art* (New York: Oxford University Press, 1989), 13.

16 Longinus, Cassius, and Herbert Allen Giles, *Longinus. An Essay on the Sublime* (London: J. Cornish & Sons, 1870), 40.

17. Ibid.

18. *Longinus, An Essay on the Sublime*, 74.

19 Andrew Ashfield and Peter De Bolla, *The Sublime: A Reader in British Eighteenth-Century Aesthetic Theory* (Cambridge University Press, 1996), 13-15.

20. Alexander Pope and S. L. Paul, *An Essay on Criticism* (Karnal: Sidhartha Publications, 1988), 39.

21. Burke, *A Philosophical Enquiry into the Origin of Our Ideas of the Sublime and Beautiful*, 58.

22. Burke, *A Philosophical Enquiry into the Origin of Our Ideas of the Sublime and Beautiful*, 7.

24. Ibid., 31.

25. Ibid., 310.

26. Ibid., 119.

27 Burke, *A Philosophical Enquiry into the Origin of Our Ideas of the Sublime and Beautiful*, 120.

28. Immanuel Kant and James Creed Meredith, *The Critique of Judgment* (Oxford: Clarendon, 1952), 103.

29. Ibid., 61.

30. Ibid., 52.

31. Ibid., 51.

32. Kant, *The Critique of Judgment*, 132.

33. Ibid.

34. Kant, *The Critique of Judgment*, 64.

35. Nicolson, *Mountain Gloom and Mountain Glory*, 15.

36. Ibid., 361.

37. George Gordon Byron and Henry Lytton Bulwer, *The Complete Works of Lord Byron* (Paris: A. and W. Galignani, 1835), 131.

38. Byron, *The Complete Works of Lord Byron*, 131.

39 Percy Shelley and Newell F. Ford, *The Poetical Works of Shelley* (Boston: Houghton Mifflin, 1975), 196.

40. Shelley, *Frankenstein, Or, The Modern Prometheus*, 76.

41. Ibid.

42. William Cronon, *Uncommon Ground: Toward Reinventing Nature* (New York: W.W. Norton & Co., 1995), 73.

43. David Pepper, Frank Webster, and George Revill, *Environmentalism: Critical Concepts* (London: Routledge, 2003), 101.

44. Clements R. Markham and F. H. H. Guillemard, *The Lands of Silence; a History of Arctic and Antarctic Exploration* (Cambridge: University Press, 1921), 3.

45. Hermann Wittenberg, *The Sublime, Imperialism and the African Landscape* (South Africa: University of the Western Cape, 2004), 16.

46. Back, *Narrative of an Expedition in HMS Terror*, 190.

47. Back, *Narrative of an Expedition in HMS Terror*, 190.

48. George Back, C. Stuart Houston, I. S. MacLaren, and Rupert's Land Record Society, *Arctic Artist: The Journal and Paintings of George Back, Midshipman With Franklin* (Buffalo: McGill-Queen's University Press, 1994), 1819-1822, 303.

49. Ibid.

50 James W. Buel, *The World's Wonders as Seen by the Great Tropical and Polar Explorers* (St. Louis: Historical Pub. Co., 1884), 589.

51. "Departure of the "Erebus" and "Terror" on the Arctic Expedition," 1.

III

1. Scott Peeples, *Edgar Allan Poe Revisited* (New York: Twayne Publisher, 1998), 55.

2. Edgar Allan Poe, *The Narrative of Arthur Gordon Pym of Nantucket* (Raleigh, N.C.: Alex Catalogue, 1990), 172.

3. Ibid., 171.

4. "The Polar Regions," *The Penny Illustrated News*, March 9, 1850, 154.

5. Glasberg, *Antarctica as Cultural Critique*, 66.

6. Douglas Mawson, *The Home of the Blizzard: Being the Story of the Australasian Antarctic Expedition, 1911-1914* (London: Hodder and Stoughton, 1930), 88.

7. Loomis, "The Arctic Sublime," 111.

8. Pierre Berton, *The Arctic Grail: The Quest for the North West Passage and the North Pole, 1818-1909* (New York, NY: Lyons, 2000), 267-268.

9. Ibid.

10. Alfred Tennyson, *The Complete Poetical Works of Tennyson* (Boston: Houghton Mifflin Publishing: 1947), 487.

11. Charles Dickens, *The Centenary Edition of the Works of Charles Dickens*, (London: Chapman & Hall, 1910), 502.

12. F. B. Maggs, *Voyages and Travels in All Parts of the World: A Descriptive Catalogue*, (London: Maggs Bros., 1962), 502.

13. Ibid.

14. Spufford. *I May Be Some Time*, 188.

15. "Departure of the "Erebus" and "Terror" on the Arctic Expedition," 6.

16. Ken McGoogan, *Lady Franklin's Revenge* (London: Bantam Press, 2006) 395; "Man Proposes, God Disposes," *The Art-Journal*, 1864, 168.

17. Buel, *The World's Wonders as Seen by the Great Tropical and Polar Explorers*, 589.

18. Jules Verne, *The Voyages and Adventures of Captain Hatteras* (Westport, Conn.: Associated Booksellers, 1961), 402.

19. Verne, *The Voyages and Adventures of Captain Hatteras*, 423.

20. Ibid., 439.

21. Ibid.

22. Back, *Narrative of an Expedition in HMS Terror*, 189.

23 George Wallace Melville, *In the Lena Delta: A Narrative of the Search for Lieut.-Commander De Long and His Companions* (Boston: Houghton, Mifflin and Co., 1885), 454.

24. Loomis, "The Arctic Sublime," 112.

25. Loomis, "The Arctic Sublime," 110.

26. Fussell, *The Great War in Modern Memory*, 258.

27. Mawson, *The Home of the Blizzard*, 88.

28. Friedrich Nietzsche, *The Gay Science* (New York: Cambridge University Press, 2001), xi.

29. Ibid.

30. James McNeill *Whistler, "Ten o'clock": A Lecture* (Portland, Me.: Thomas Bird Mosher, 1916), 14.

31. Whistler, *"Ten o'clock": A Lecture*, 15.

32. T.S. Eliot, *The Waste Land: A Facsimile and Transcript of the Original Drafts Including the Annotations of Ezra Pound* (New York: Harcourt Brace Jovanovich, 1971), 61.

33. Ibid.

34. Ibid.

35. Bill Manhire, *The Wide White Page: Writers Imagine Antarctica* (Wellington, N.Z.: Victoria University Press, 2004), 115.

36. Ibid., 123.

37. Manhire, *The Wide White Page*, 123.

38. H.P. Lovecraft, *At the Mountains of Madness* (New York: Modern Library, 2005), 28.

39. Ibid.

40 Ibid.

41. Lovecraft, *At the Mountains of Madness*, 96.

42. Ibid.

43. Charles Laseron, *South with Mawson; Reminiscences of the Australasian Antarctic Expedition, 1911-1914* (London: G.G. Harrap, 1947), 36.

44. Laseron, *South with Mawson; Reminiscences of the Australasian Antarctic Expedition*, 36.

45. Shackleton, South, 1.

IV

1. H.D. Rawnsley, "In Honour of Captain Scott," *British Review*, April 1913, 81.

2. Max Jones, *The Last Great Quest: Captain Scott's Antarctic Sacrifice* (Oxford: Oxford University Press, 2004), 142.

3. Mawson, *The Home of the Blizzard*, 88.

4. "Departure of the "Erebus" and "Terror" on the Arctic Expedition," 6.

5. Tom Griffiths, *Slicing the Silence: Voyaging to Antarctica* (England: Harvard University Press, 2007), 11.

6. Griffiths, *Slicing the Silence*, 11.

7. John Tosh, *A Man's Place: Masculinity and the Middle-class Home in Victorian England* (New Haven: Yale University Press, 2007), 171-172.

8. Barczewski, *Antarctic Destinies*, xii.

9. Ibid., xii, 146.

10. "Second Leader," *The Illustrated London News*, October 1, 1859, 316.

11. "Hero Caught in an Icy Blast," *The Times*, February 11, 1985, 12.

12. Ernest Shackleton, *The Heart of the Antarctic: Being the Story of the British Antarctic Expedition, 1907-1909* (New York: Carroll & Graf Publishers, 1999), ix.

13. Loomis, *"The Arctic Sublime,"* 95.

14. Ernest Shackleton, *Aurora Australis: 1908-09* (Ramsbury, UK: Airlife Publishing Ltd., 1989), 80.

15. Shackleton, South, 344.

16. Ibid.

17. Mawson, *The Home of the Blizzard*, 88.

18. Ibid.

19. Aurora Peak is located alongside of the Mertz Glacier, just south of Mount Murchison. The peak was discovered by Mawson and named after the expedition ship Aurora.

20. Mawson, *The Home of the Blizzard*, 235.

21. Shackleton, South, 173.

22. Leonard Darwin, "Luncheon to British Antarctic Expedition," *Geographical Journal*, 1910, 36.

23. Ibid.

24. Arthur Conan Doyle, *Through the Magic Door* (Charleston: BiblioBazaar, 2006), 93.

25. Nancy Flannery, *This Everlasting Silence: The Love Letters of Paquita Delprat and Douglas Mawson, 1911-1914* (Melbourne: Melbourne UP, 2005), 102.

26. Flannery, *This Everlasting Silence*, 67.

27. Regina W. Daly, *The Shackleton Letters: Behind the Scenes of the "Nimrod" Expedition* (Norwich: The Erskine Press, 2010), 308.

28. Peggy Pegrine, "A letter of application to join Ernest Shackleton's Endurance expedition" (Scott Polar Research Institute: University of Cambridge, UK).

29. Frank Wild, "Rejection letter to Peggy Pegrine" (Scott Polar Research Institute: University of Cambridge, UK).

30. "Mawson Antarctic Expedition: 25 Female Applicants," The Times, July 6, 1929, 13.

31. Ibid.

32. Ibid.

33. Tosh, *A Man's Place*, 171-172.

34. Ibid., 172-174.

35. Ibid., 172.

36. Doyle, *Through the Magic Door*, 93.

37. Tosh, *A Man's Place*, 174.

38. Caroline Alexander, *The Endurance: Shackleton's Legendary Antarctic Expedition* (New York: Knopf, 1998), 193.

39. Tosh, *A Man's Place*, 177.

40. Mary Jo Gohlke, *Remarkable Women of Stockton* (Charleston, SC: The History Press, 2014), 54; "Woman Explorer's Hazardous Trip In South America," *The New York Times*, August 18, 2012.

41. Gohlke, *Remarkable Women of Stockton*, 58.

42. Mina Hubbard, Roberta Buchanan, Anne Hart, and B. A. Greene, *Woman Who Mapped Labrador: The Life and Expedition Diary of Mina Hubbard* (Montreal: McGill-Queen's University Press, 2005), 9.

43. Hubbard, Buchanan, Hart, and Greene, *Woman Who Mapped Labrador*, 9.

44. Ibid.

45. Mina Hubbard, *A Woman's Way through Unknown Labrador* (Montreal: McGill-Queen's University Press, 2004), 90.

46. Ibid., 188.

47. Hubbard, *A Woman's Way through Unknown Labrador*, 83, 44, 60, 72.

48. Robert Falcon Scott, *Scott's Last Expedition: The Journals* (Oxford: Oxford University Press, 2005), 171.

49. Barczewski, *Antarctic Destinies*, 145.

50. Barczewski, *Antarctic Destinies*, 146.

51. "Antarctic Disaster: Loss of Captain Scott and His Party," *The Times*, February 11, 1913.

52. Scott, *Scott's Last Expedition*, 416.

53. Ibid.

54. "A Polar Epic," *Daily Chronicle*, February 12, 1913, 6.

55. "Tragedy of the South Pole, *Daily Graphic*, February 11, 1913, 4.

56. "Scott's Last Expedition," *The Times*, November 6, 1913, 6.

57. *Evening News*, February 12, 1913, 1.

58. Robert Falcon Scott, *Captain Scott's Message to England* (London: St. Catherine's Press, 1913), 30.

59. *Evening News*, February 12, 1913, 1.

60. R. Baden-Powell, "Scout Yarns," *Scout*, November 22, 1913, 266.

61. Ibid.

62. "Well Done!," *Daily Mail*, February 14, 1913, 4.

63. A. Machen, "The Immortal Story of Captain Scott's Expedition–How Five Brave Englishmen Died," 1913, 1.

64. Ibid, 2.

65. "Captain Scott's Memorial," *The Times*, May 6, 1916, 5.

66. *Natural Science: A Monthly Review of Scientific Progress*, vol. 14 (London: Young J. Pentland, 1899), 418.

67. "Statue to Sir John Franklin," *The Times*, November 16, 1866, 10.

68. "Shackleton's Burial 'At the Gate of the Antarctic'," *The Times*, May 29, 1922, 14.

69. "Nation's Tribute to Shackleton," *The Times*, March 3, 1922, 14.

70. C.P. Conigrave, "Sir Ernest Shackleton," *Northern Territory Times and Gazette*, February 4, 1922, 3.

71. William Henry Davenport Adams, *The Arctic World: Its Plants, Animals, and Natural Phenomena* (London: T. Nelson and Sons, 1876), 2.

72. Loomis, "The Arctic Sublime," 99.

73. "Antarctic Disaster: The Loss of Captain Scott and His Party," The Times, February 11, 1913.; "Statue of Sir John Franklin," *The Times*, November 16, 1866.; C. P. Conigrave, "Sir Ernest Shackleton," *Northern Territory Times and Gazette*, February 4, 1922.

74. Joseph Conrad, *The Heart of Darkness* (New York: Dover Publications, 1990), 2.

75. Lovecraft, *At the Mountains of Madness*, 28.

76. Ibid., 28.

V

1. "Tending Sir Ernest's Legacy: An Interview with Alexandra Shackleton." NOVA Online. February 1, 2002. Accessed May 16, 2018. http://www.pbs.org/wgbh/nova/shackleton/1914/alexandra.html.

2. "The Union Jack's Travels," *The Times*, May 31, 1917, 3.

3. "British Triumph in the South Polar Regions," *The Daily Mirror*, May 11, 1909, 1.

4. "Antarctic Disaster: Loss of Captain Scott and His Party," *The Times*, February 11, 1913.

5. Fussell, *The Great War in Modern Memory*, 12.

6. Eric J. Leed, *No Man's Land: Combat & Identity in World War I* (Cambridge University Press, 1979), 10.

7. Leed, *No Man's Land: Combat & Identity in World War I*, 108.

8. Fran Brearton, *The Great War in Irish Poetry: W.B. Yeats to Michael* Longley (Oxford University Press, 2000), 253.

9. Ibid., 253.

10. Fussell

11. Hill, *White Horizon*, 2.

12. Fussell, *The Great War in Modern Memory*, 12.

13. Ibid., 217.

14. Ibid., 12.

15. Spufford, *I May Be Some Time*, 6.

16. Charles Carrington, *Soldier from the Wars Returning* (New York: McKay, 1965), 87.

17. Mawson, *The Home of the Blizzard*, 235.

18. Ardern Arthur Hulme Beaman, *The Squadroon* (New York: John Lane Company, 1920), 187.

19. Osbert Sitwell, *Laughter in the Next Room* (Boston: Little, Brown, 1948), 8.

20. Wilfred Owen, *The Collected Poems of Wilfred Owen* (New York: New Directions, 1964), 160.

WORKS CITED

Primary Sources

———. "A Monstrous Conception." *The Times*, August 25, 1982.

———. "A Polar Epic." *Daily Chronicle*, February 12, 1913.

Adams, William Henry Davenport. *The Arctic World: Its Plants, Animals, and Natural Phenomena*. London: T. Nelson and Sons, 1876.

Alexander, Caroline. *The Endurance: Shackleton's Legendary Antarctic Expedition*. New York: Knopf, 1998.

———. "Antarctic Disaster: The Loss of Captain Scott and His Party." *The Times*, February 11, 1913.

Appleman, Philip. *1859: Entering an Age of Crisis*. Bloomington: Indiana University Press, 1959.

Back, George. *The Narrative of an Expedition in HMS Terror: Undertaken with a View to Geographic Discovery on the Arctic Shores, 1836-7*. New York: Cambridge University Press, 2013.

Back, George. *Coppermine Mouth*, 1821. Watercolor on canvas. Library and Archives Canada, W.H. Coverdale Collection of Canadiana.

Back, George, C. Stuart Houston, I. S. MacLaren, and Rupert's Land Record Society. *Arctic Artist: The Journal and Paintings of George Back, Midshipman With Franklin*. Buffalo: McGill-Queen's University Press, 1994.

Baden-Powell, R. "Scout Yarns," *Scout*. November 22, 1913.

Balme, Jennifer Hobhouse and Emily Hobhouse. *To Love One's Enemies: The Work and Life of Emily Hobhouse Compiled from Letters and Writings, Newspaper Cuttings and Official Documents*. Cobble Hill, Canada: Hobhouse Trust, 1994.

Barrow, John. *The American Review: A Whig Journal of Politics, Literature, Art, and Science*, Volumes 11-12. New York: Wiley and Putnam, 1850.

Beaman, Ardern Arthur Hulme. *The Squadroon*. New York: John Lane Company, 1920.

Boehmer, Elleke. *Empire Writing: An Anthology of Colonial Literature, 1870-1918* .New York: Oxford University Press, 1998.

Brearton, Fran. *The Great War in Irish Poetry: W.B. Yeats to Michael Longley*. Oxford University Press, 2000.

————"British Triumph in the South Polar Regions." *The Daily Mirror*, May 11, 1909.

Buel, James W. *The World's Wonders as Seen by the Great Tropical and Polar Explorers*. St. Louis: Historical Pub. Co., 1884.

Burke, Edmund. *A Philosophical Enquiry into the Origin of Our Ideas of the Sublime and Beautiful*. New York: Oxford University Press, 2008.

Butler, Angie, ed. T*he Quest for Frank Wild: Including his Original Memoirs*. Radway, Warwick: Jackleberry, 2011.

Byron, George Gordon and Henry Lytton Bulwer. *The Complete Works of Lord Byron*. Paris: A. and W. Galignani, 1835.

Campbell, John. *Who Goes There?* Somerset: Rocket Ride Books, 2009.

————. "Cape of Pillars, Prince Rudolf Land." *Illustrated London News*, September 11, 1875.

Carrington, Charles. *Soldier from the Wars Returning*. New York: McKay, 1965.

Conigrave, C.P. "Sir Ernest Shackleton." *Northern Territory Times and Gazette*, February 4, 1922.

Daly, Regina W., ed. *The Shackleton Letters: Behind the Scenes of the "Nimrod" Expedition*. Norwich: The Erskine Press, 2010.

Darwin, Leonard. "Luncheon to British Antarctic Expedition." *Geographical Journal*, 1910.

————. "Departure of the "Erebus" and "Terror" on the Arctic Expedition." *London News*, May 19, 1845.

Dickens, Charles. *The Centenary Edition of the Works of Charles Dickens*. London: N.P., 1910.

Doyle, Arthur Conan. *Through the Magic Door*. Charleston: Biblio Bazaar, 2006.

Eliot, T.S. *The Waste Land: A Facsimile and Transcript of the Original Drafts Including the Annotations of Ezra Pound*. New York: Harcourt Brace Jovanovich, 1971.

Flannery, Nancy. *This Everlasting Silence: The Love Letters of Paquita Delprat and Douglas Mawson, 1911-1914*. Melbourne: Melbourne UP, 2005.

———. "Hero Caught in an Icy Blast." *The Times*, February 11, 1985.

Hobhouse, Emily and Ruth Fry, *Emily Hobhouse: A Memoir*. London: J. Cape, 1929.

Hubbard, Mina. *A Woman's Way through Unknown Labrador*. Montreal: McGill-Queen's University Press, 2004.

Kant, Immanuel and James Creed Meredith. *The Critique of Judgment*. Oxford: Clarendon, 1952.

Kingsley, Charles. *The Works of Charles Kingsley*. Philadelphia: John D. Morris & Co., 1899.

Kipling, Rudyard. *Rudyard Kipling: Poems*. New York: Everyman's Library, 2007.

Lancaster, Bill. *The Thing, 1981 Screenplay by Bill Lancaster*. University Reprint, 2012.

Landseer, Edwin. *Man Proposes, God Disposes*, 1864. Oil on canvas, Royal Holloway College, University of London.

Lawrence, T.E. *Seven Pillars of Wisdom*. Hertfordshire: Wordsworth Editions Ltd., 1997.

Longinus, Cassius, and Herbert Allen Giles, *Longinus. An Essay on the Sublime*. London: J. Cornish & Sons, 1870.

Lovecraft, H.P. *At the Mountains of Madness*. New York: Modern Library, 2005.

Machen, A. "The Immortal Story of Captain Scott's Expedition–How Five Brave Englishmen Died." 1913.

Maggs, F. B. *Voyages and Travels in All Parts of the World: A Descriptive Catalogue*. London: Maggs Bros., 1962.

Manhire, Bill. *The Wide White Page: Writers Imagine Antarctica*. Wellington, N.Z.: Victoria University Press, 2004.

Mawson, Douglas. *The Home of the Blizzard: Being the Story of the Australasian Antarctic Expedition, 1911-1914*. London: Hodder and Stoughton, 1930.

Markham, Clements R. and F. H. H. Guillemard. *The Lands of Silence; a History of Arctic and Antarctic Exploration*. Cambridge: University Press, 1921.

Melville, George Wallace. *In the Lena Delta: A Narrative of the Search for Lieut.-Commander De Long and His Companions*. Boston: Houghton, Mifflin and Co., 1885.

Millais, Sir John Everett. *The North-West Passage, 1874*. Tate Modern Art Museum.

Nietzsche, Friedrich, *The Gay Science*. Cambridge University Press, 2001.

O'Reilly, Mary Boyle. "Story of Woman Who Waited." *The Tacoma Times*, June 01, 1916.

Orwell, George. *A Collection of Essays*. New York: Mariner Books, 1970.

Owen, Wilfred. *The Collected Poems of Wilfred Owen*. New York: New Directions, 1964.

Poe, Edgar Allan. *The Narrative of Arthur Gordon Pym of Nantucket*. Raleigh, N.C.: Alex Catalogue, 1990.

Pope, Alexander and S. L. Paul. *An Essay on Criticism*. Karnal: Sidhartha Publications, 1988.

Scarborough, Harold E. "Two Boy Scouts Explore Antarctic." *New-York Tribune*, September 11, 1921.

———. "Second Leader." *The Illustrated London News*. October 1, 1859.

Stanley, Arthur Penrhyn. *The Life and Correspondence of Thomas Arnold*, Volume 2. New York: Philadelphia, G.S. Appleton.

Scott, Robert Falcon. *Scott's Last Expedition: The Journals*. Oxford: Oxford University Press, 2005.

Scott, Robert Falcon. *Captain Scott's Message to England*. St. Catherine's Press, 1913.

――――. "Scott's Last Expedition." *The Times*, November 6, 1913.

Shackleton, Ernest Henry, George Marston, and Mary P. Goodwin. *Aurora Australis: 1908-09*. Ramsbury, UK: Airlife Publishing Ltd., 1989.

Shackleton, Ernest Henry. *South: The Endurance Expedition*. New York: Signet, 1999.

Shackleton, Ernest Henry. *The Heart of the Antarctic: Being the Story of the British Antarctic Expedition, 1907-1909*. New York: Carroll & Graf Publishers, 1999.

Shelley, *Mary. Frankenstein, or The Modern Prometheus*. Lancaster: Sovereign, 2012.

Shelley, Percy and Newell F. Ford. *The Poetical Works of Shelley*. Boston: Houghton Mifflin, 1975.

Sitwell, Osbert. *Laughter in the Next Room*. Boston: Little, Brown, 1948.

Smith, Thomas. *Franklin's Last Expedition*, 1864. Oil on canvas, National Maritime Museum, Greenwich, London

South. Directed by Frank Hurley. 1919. London: BFI, 2002. DVD.

――――. "Speech to the Cobden Club denouncing the Brussels sugar convention." *The Times*, November, 29 1902.

Tennyson, Alfred. *The Complete Poetical Works of Tennyson*. Boston: Houghton Mifflin Publishing: 1947.

———. "South-African War Mortality." *The Parliamentary Debates: Fourth Series, Second Season of the Twenty-Seventh Parliament if the United Kingdom of Great Britain and Ireland*. Fetter Lane, London: Wyman and Sons. 1901.

———. "The Polar Regions." *The Penny Illustrated News*, March 9, 1850.

Rawnsley, H.D. "In Honour of Captain Scott." *British Review*, April 1913.

———. "The Return of the Thing that Stalked the Thirties." *The Times*, August 20th, 1982.

———. "The Thing, Horror, and Science Fiction." *New York Times*, June 25th, 1982.

———. "The Union Jack's Travels." *The Times*, May 31, 1917.

———. "Tragedy of the South Pole." *Daily Graphic*, February 11, 1913.

———."Tending Sir Ernest's Legacy: An Interview with Alexandra Shackleton." NOVA Online. February 1, 2002. Accessed March 5, 2015. http://www.pbs.org/wgbh/nova/shackleton/1914/alexandra.html.

Verne, Jules. *The Voyages and Adventures of Captain Hatteras*. Westport, Conn.: Associated Booksellers, 1961.

———. "Well Done!" *Daily Mail*. February 14, 1913.

Wheeler, Sara. *The Magnetic North: Notes from the Arctic Circle.* New York: Farrar, Strauss and Giroux, 2011.

Whistler, James McNeill. *"Ten o'clock": A Lecture.* Portland, Me.: Thomas Bird Mosher, 1916.

Wild, Frank. *Shackleton's Last Voyage.* London: Cassell, 1923.

———. "Woman Explorer's Hazardous Trip in South America." *The New York Times.* August 18, 2012.

Worsley, Frank Arthur. *Shackleton's Boat Journey: the Narrative from the Captain of the Endurance.* Wyoming: The Narrative Press, 2001.

Secondary Sources

Alexander, Caroline. *The Endurance: Shackleton's Legendary Antarctic Expedition.* New York: Knopf, 1998.

Ashfield, Andrew and Peter De Bolla. *The Sublime: A Reader in British Eighteenth-Century Aesthetic Theory.* Cambridge University Press, 1996.

Barczewski, Stephanie L. *Antarctic Destinies: Scott, Shackleton and the Changing Face of Heroism.* New York: Continuum, 2008.

Barraclough, Geoffrey. *An Introduction to Contemporary History.* New York: Basic Books, 1965.

Berton, Pierre. *The Arctic Grail: The Quest for the North West Passage and the North Pole, 1818-1909*. New York, NY: Lyons, 2000.

Brendon, Piers. *The Decline and Fall of the British Empire, 1781-1997*. New York: Alfred A. Knopf, 2008.

Brown, Stephen. *The Last Viking: The Life of Roald Amundsen*. Vancouver: D&M Publishers Incorporated, 2012.

Carter, Paul. *The Road to Botany Bay: An Exploration of Landscape and History*. New York: Knopf, 1988.

Cavell, Janice. *Tracing the Connected Narrative: Arctic Exploration in British Print Culture, 1818-1860*. Toronto: University of Toronto Press, 2008.

Colley, Linda. *Britons: Forging the Nation, 1707-1837*. New Haven : Yale University Press, 1992.

Crowther, Paul. *The Kantian Sublime: From Morality to Art*. New York: Oxford University Press, 1989.

David, Robert G. *The Arctic in the British Imagination, 1818-1914*. Manchester: Manchester University Press, 2000.

Driver, Felix. *Geography Militant: Cultures of Exploration and Empire*. New York: Blackwell Publishers, 2001.

Edney, Matthew H. *Mapping an Empire: the Geographical Construction of British India, 1765-184*3. Chicago: University Of Chicago Press, 1999..

Ferguson, Niall. Empire: *The Rise and Demise of the British World Order and the Lessons for Global Power.* New York: Basic Books, 2003.

Fisher, Margery and James Fisher. *Shackleton.* London: Barrie, 1957.

Foucault, Michel and Jeremy W Crampton. *Space, Knowledge and Power: Foucault and Geography.* Burlington, VT: Ashgate, 2007.

Fussell, Paul. *The Great War in Modern Memory.* Oxford University Press, 1975.

Glasberg, Elena. *Antarctica as Cultural Critique: The Gendered Politics of Scientific Exploration and Climate Change.* New York: Palgrave Macmillan, 2012.

Gohlke, Mary Jo. *Remarkable Women of Stockton.* Charleston, SC: The History Press, 2014.

Gooch, John. *The Boer War: Direction, Experience and Image.* Portland Frank Cass, 2000.

Graham, Lorrie and Tim Wilson. "Questions of Being: Am Exploration of Enduring Dreams." *In Echoing Silence: Essays on Arctic Narrative*, edited by Gerald Lynch, 137-143. Ottawa: University of Ottawa Press, 1997.

Griffiths, Tom. *Slicing the Silence: Voyaging to Antarctica.* England: Harvard University Press, 2007.

Hill, Jen. "A Pale Blank of Mist and Cloud: Arctic Spaces in Jane Eyre." *In White Horizon*, edited by Pamela K. Gilbert, 89-111. Albany: State University of New York, 2008.

Hill, Jen. "A Propitious Hard Frost: The Arctic of Mary Shelley and Eleanor Anne Porden." *In White Horizon*, edited by Pamela K. Gilbert, 53-87. Albany: State University of New York, 2008.

Hill, Jen. "Heart of Whiteness." In *White Horizon*, edited by Pamela K. Gilbert, 1-28. Albany: State University of New York, 2008.

Hitt, Christopher. "Toward an Ecological Sublime." *New Literary History*, Vol. 30, No. 3 (1999).

Hubbard, Mina, Roberta Buchanan, Anne Hart, and B. A. Greene. *Woman Who Mapped Labrador: The Life and Expedition Diary of Mina Hubbard*. Montreal: McGill-Queen's University Press, 2005.

Huntford, Roland. *Shackleton*. New York: Carroll & Graf, 1998.

Jones, Max. *The Last Great Quest: Captain Scott's Antarctic Sacrifice*. Oxford: Oxford University Press, 2004.

Kennedy, Dane. "British Exploration in the Nineteenth Century: A Historiographical Survey." *History Compass* 5, no. 6 (2007): 1879-1900.

Kennedy, Dane. *Britain and Empire, 1880-1945*. Harlow : Longman, 2002.

Krans, Michael. "Writing For an Elsewhere: Author(ity) and Authenticity in the Texts of the First Franklin Expedition (1819-1822)." *Studies in Canadian Literature* Vol. 24, No. 1 (1999): 9.

Larson, Edward J. *An Empire of Ice: Scott, Shackleton, and the Heroic age of Antarctic Science*. New Haven: Yale University Press, 2011.

Leed, Eric J. *No Man's Land: Combat & Identity in World War I*. Cambridge University Press, 1979.

Levine, George."Ruskin and the Novelists," in *Nature and the Victorian Imagination*, ed. U. C. Knoepflmacher. Berkeley: University of California Press, 1977.

Loomis, Chauncey C. "The Arctic Sublime," in *Nature and the Victorian Imagination*, ed. U. C. Knoepflmacher. Berkeley: University of California Press, 1977.

Ludecke, Cornelia. "Scientific Collaboration in Antarctica (1901-04): A Challenge in Times of Political Rivalry." *Polar Record* 39, no. 1 (2003): 35-48.

MacKenzie, John M. *Imperialism and Popular Culture*. Manchester, UK; Dover, N.H., 1986.

MacLaren, I. S. "The Aesthetic Map of the North, 1845-1859." *Arctic Institute of North America* Vol. 38, No. 2 (1985): 101.

Marlow, James. "English Cannibalism: Dickens after 1859." *Studies in English Literature, 1500-1900* Vol. 23, No. 4 (1983): 652.

Martin, Constance. "Science as Poetic and Visual Narrative: J. Dewey Soper (1893-1982)." *In Echoing Silence: Essays on Arctic Narrative*, edited by Gerald Lynch, 61-67. Ottawa: University of Ottawa Press, 1997.

Massey, Doreen. *For Space*. London: SAGE Publications Ltd, 2005.

Mills, William James. *Exploring Polar Frontiers: A Historical Encyclopedia, Volume 1*. Oxford: ABC-Clio, 2003.

Nicolson, Marjorie. *Mountain Gloom and Mountain Glory; the Development of the Aesthetics of the Infinite*. Ithaca, NY: Cornell UP, 1959.

Parsons, Timothy. *The British Imperial Century, 1815-1914: A World History Perspective*. Lanham, Md.: Rowman & Littlefield, 1999.

Peeples, Scott. *Edgar Allan Poe Revisited*. New York: Twayne Publisher, 1998.

Pepper, David, Frank Webster, and George Revill. *Environmentalism: Critical Concepts*. London: Routledge, 2003.

Spufford, Francis. *I May Be Some Time: Ice and the English Imagination*. New York: St. Martin's, 1997.

Said, Edward W. Orientalism. New York: Vintage Books, 2008.

Taylor, Miles. *Southampton: Gateway to the British Empire*. England: I. B. Tauris, 2007.

Tosh, John. *A Man's Place: Masculinity and the Middle-class Home in Victorian England*. New Haven: Yale University Press, 2007.

Wilson, Kathleen. *The Island Race: Englishness, Empire, and Gender in the Eighteenth Century*. New York: Routledge, 2003.

Wittenberg, Hermann. *The Sublime, Imperialism and the African Landscape*. South Africa: University of the Western Cape, 2004.

www.ingramcontent.com/pod-product-compliance
Lightning Source LLC
Chambersburg PA
CBHW021818170526
45157CB00007B/2630